TH

WO

WITH THE

FLYING HEAD

AND OTHER STORIES
BY KURAHASHI YUMIKO

A series edited by
Michiko Niikuni Wilson

Japanese Women Writing, devoted to works by and about Japanese literary women, celebrates the resurgence of women's writings in a country that gave women a voice and a room of their own as early as A.D. 900. Despite a long hiatus in the female literary tradition between 1190 and 1868, and another during the Pacific War, Japanese female writers have been able to reclaim what is their due. Introducing a wide range of writing since the early 1900s—fiction, poetry, critical essays, and biographies—**Japanese Women Writing** attempts to redefine the modern Japanese literary canon and highlight a female perspective that intersects with the notions of gender, power, and sexuality.

THE WOMAN WITH THE FLYING HEAD

AND OTHER STORIES BY KURAHASHI YUMIKO

TRANSLATED BY ATSUKO SAKAKI

An East Gate Book

M. E. Sharpe
Armonk, New York
London, England

An East Gate Book

The publisher gratefully acknowledges the support of the Association for 100 Japanese Books, which provided a grant to support the publication of this book.

Library of Congress Cataloging-in-Publication Data

Kurahashi, Yumiko, 1935–
The woman with the flying head and other stories / by Kurahashi Yumiko;
translated by Atsuko Sakaki
p. cm.—(Japanese women writing)
Contents: An extraterrestrial—We are lovers—The house of the black cat—
The woman with the flying head—The trade—The witch mask—Spring night dreams—
The passage of dreams—A special place—Flower abstraction—
The long passage of dreams
ISBN 0-7656-0157-5 (cloth : alk. paper). ISBN 0-7656-0158-3 (paper : alk. paper)
1. Kurahashi, Yumiko,–1935—Translations into English.
I. Sakaki, Atsuko, 1963– . II. Title. III. Series.
PL855.U6A26 1997
895.6′35—dc21 97-19074
CIP

Printed in the United States of America

The paper used in this publication meets the minimum requirements of
American National Standard for Information Sciences—
Permanence of Paper for Printed Library Materials,
ANSI Z 39.48-1984.

∞

BM (c) 10 9 8 7 6 5 4 3 2 1
BM (p) 10 9 8 7 6 5 4 3 2

For Him Inside Me

Contents

Acknowledgments

My journey toward this anthology had its origin in the Ph.D. dissertation which I submitted to the University of British Columbia in July 1992, entitled "The Intertextual Novel and the Interrelational Self: Kurahashi Yumiko, a Japanese Postmodernist." Though the dissertation includes no complete translation of any of Kurahashi's stories, I discuss them in the introduction, and chapter 4 deals in part with the last story in this volume, "The Long Passage of Dreams." My primary advisor, Kinya Tsuruta, commented then that he found my thesis more interesting to read than Kurahashi's stories, an impression I hope—with due gratitude for his tolerance and support of my scholarly work—to challenge with this volume.

Thanks to the understanding shown by my senior colleagues in the Japanese literature program at Harvard, Jay Rubin and Edwin Cranston, and then chairs of the department Stephen Owen and Harold Bolitho, I was able to teach "Nagai yumeji" ["The Long Passage of Dreams"] in the spring of 1993 and the fall of 1995 in a course for close reading called Japanese Literature 108. It is with delight and pleasant memories that I mention the names of the students enrolled in the course, to whom I owe a great deal: Lena Akai, Peter Carolan, Charo D'Etcheverry, David Greenspan, Sean Hennessey, Yoko Kiser, Sergio Reyes, Nathan Scales, and Joan Siegel. They will see reincarnations of their translation assignments in the current version of "The Long Passage of Dreams." I am of course responsible for any errors or problems that might remain. The enthusiasm shown by the majority of the students convinced me that Kurahashi's fiction could indeed provoke and engage a wide range of readers.

I would never have planned to publish my translations, however, if it had not been for the encouragement of Stephen Owen, who responded enthusiastically to draft translations of some of the stories based on Chinese literary sources and gave generously of his time, offering support as well as stylistic suggestions. I cannot thank him enough for his kindness. It was most fortunate that I was able to count on the editorial help of Robert Ashmore, who proofread the manuscript and gave thorough and thoughtful suggestions for further polishing. Without his help, this volume would never have been possible.

I would like to also thank the following institutions and organizations, which have given me opportunities to present my ideas on Kurahashi Yumiko and alerted me to the existence of many potential readers: the Department of Asian Studies, University of British Columbia (1992, 1995); the Department of East Asian Languages and Civilizations, Harvard University (1993); the Department of East Asian Languages and Center for Japanese Studies, University of California, Berkeley (1993); the Department of East Asian Studies, University of Toronto (1994); the International Comparative Literature Association (1994); the Edwin O. Reischauer Institute for Japanese Studies (1996); and the Association for Asian Studies Pacific Coast Regional Conference (1996). I am particularly thrilled by the positive response with constructive comments of Sharalyn Orbaugh, Kenneth L. Richard, and Howard Hibbett. I am also thankful to Rebecca Copeland, Esperanza Ramirez-Christensen, Philip Gabriel, and Stephen Snyder who, having extensively commented on my papers on Kurahashi, implicitly or explicitly showed strong interest in Kurahashi's fiction.

I am especially grateful for Michiko Niikuni Wilson, who, as editor of the series *Japanese Women Writing,* read the manuscript, made helpful suggestions, and gave her support to the project. I am also indebted to Douglas Merwin for sharing my enthusiasm for the stories, and for offering his editorial expertise. Mai Shaikhanuar-Cota and Angela Piliouras have been very kind as, step after step, I approached the completion of the project. On the Japan side, Kurita Akiko of the Japan Foreign-Rights Centre responded immediately and positively to my primary contact, which relieved me of any psychological obstacle I faced as a novice in the business of translation. I was most astonished and excited by a phone call from Kurahashi Yumiko herself, who compared my papers on her to "surgical operations which revealed the anatomy of my body and which made me feel as if cool winds had blown through my body" and showed support and enthusiasm for this project. It was a metafictional moment, in which author and reader encountered each other in reality!

Finally, I am pleased to be able to show this volume to my parents. The publication project materialized when my father was recovering from illness, nursed by my mother. Unlike the father in "The Long Passage of Dreams," he is well now and able to see his daughter's publication in the United States.

I gratefully acknowledge financial support for the completion of this project from the Junior Faculty Work-Study Program, Faculty of Arts and Sciences, and the Japan Fund, Department of East Asian Languages and Civilizations, both of Harvard University.

Introduction

Atsuko Sakaki

Kurahashi Yumiko (b. 1935) has enlivened the Japanese literary scene since 1960, when she made her debut in the mass media with "Parutai" (trans. "Partei"). This short story, in which a female college student makes detached observations about her lover and about a political party she joins, caused Hirano Ken, one of the literary "fathers" of the 1994 Nobel Prize winner Ōe Kenzaburō, to compare Kurahashi with Ōe. "Parutai" won a Meiji University President's Prize and was nominated for an Akutagawa Prize, signs that a promising career had begun. Within a year Kurahashi was nominated again for the Akutagawa Prize, this time for her "Natsu no owari" (trans. "The End of Summer"); this did not win the prize either, perhaps due to its culturally neutral portrayal of characters, whose "names" are letters of the alphabet—a characteristic of early Kurahashi fiction—and to the surreal absurdity of its murder conspiracy plot, which involves two sisters and their mutual lover K. Kurahashi was, however, awarded a Joryū bungaku shō (Women's Literature Prize) in 1961 and a Tamura Toshiko Prize in 1963 for her work as a whole.

Indeed, Kurahashi published one or two stories per month in major literary journals throughout the first few years of her career, while maintaining the qualities for which she had come to be known—most notably her skill at giving concrete form to such abstract concepts as negativity, such as one might find in the works of Franz Kafka or Abe Kōbō.

Indeed, she has been appropriately described as "one of the most fiercely intellectual writers in the contemporary scene—and also one of the most interesting and even, at times, funny" (Lyons 115). The combination of metaphysical themes with satirical touches evident throughout Kurahashi's earlier fiction was, however, often attacked by critics in the 1960s as "artificial." "Kurahashi Yumiko has been labeled a 'controversial' writer" (Aoyama 38); her work triggered several sustained debates among literary critics regarding the role of the novelist, the boundaries of literature, and strategies of composition. The norms of the time called for a fictional medium of utmost transparency, and to highlight, as Kurahashi did, the artifice or constructedness of the literary work was considered deviant.

Given that the work of male intellectual writers of a similar bent, such as Abe, while not immune to this sort of criticism, was received with more tolerance, one might infer that femaleness was conceived of as incompatible with a philosophical tone. Acclaimed women writers had most often, if not always, won approval by writing of their own emotional and physical experiences in an apparently unmediated mode, without foregrounding the art of narration. Japanese women had been even more strictly confined than Japanese men to writing "naturally" or Naturalistically, to giving vent to feelings rather than articulating thought.

Rather than simply failing to observe them, Kurahashi actively challenged such norms. She has further spoken out in a number of critical essays, most of which are collected in anthologies such as *Watashi no naka no kare e* (*For Him Inside Me*) (1970), *Meiro no tabibito* (*Traveler in a Labyrinth*) (1972), *Jishaku no nai tabi* (*Traveling Without a Compass*) (1979), *Saigo kara nibanme no dokuyaku* (*The Second-to-Last Poison*) (1986), and *Mugen no utage* (*Feast of Dreams and Illusions*) (1996), among others. Kurahashi has thus made a place for herself as a thinker as well as a creative writer. In her most frequently quoted essay, "Shōsetsu no meiro to hiteisei" (trans. "The Labyrinth and Negativity of Fiction") (1966), she defiantly renounces any imperative to represent the actual world. Instead, she declares, "[a]t an uncertain time, in a place that is nowhere, somebody who is no one, for no reason, is about to do something—and in the end does nothing: this is my ideal of the novel" (Keene 247).

Since 1964, Kurahashi has focused more on writing full-length novels, including *Sumiyakisuto Kyū no bōken* (trans. *The Adventures of Sumiyakist Q*) (1969), and *Amanon koku ōkan ki* (*Account of a Round Trip to the Amanons*) (1987), which was awarded the Izumi Kyōka Prize of that year—a reacknowledgment of Kurahashi's achievement in imaginative and fantastic literature. Apart from these two novels, however, she has seemed to lean more toward concrete description, naming characters in Japanese, and mentioning existing names of places and things. Such culturalization is often explained as the result of an existential change from the experimental to the conventional, or from the expatriate to the nationalistic Japanese—a transformation Kurahashi underwent, some scholars argue, on returning to Japan after a stay in the United States as a Fulbright artist in 1966–67. I am inclined rather to suggest that the change represents a furthering of the performativity of her work, as

Kurahashi dresses the bone structure of the absurdist archetype in the trappings of contemporary Japanese society, or of neoclassicist reinventions of scenes from classical literary sources.

A similar change is apparent in her short stories. Kurahashi did publish several anthologies of short stories, such as *Otona no tame no zankoku dōwa* (*Cruel Fairy Tales for Adults*) (1984), *Kurahashi Yumiko no kaiki shōhen* (*Horror Stories by Kurahashi Yumiko*) (1985), *Yume no kayoiji* (*The Passage of Dreams*) (1989), and *Gensō kaigakan* (*Fantastic Gallery*) (1991). Her satirical touch intact if not sharpened, the immediately identifiable sources are more diversified: in addition to Kafka and other experimentalists, classical tales of the East and West are pastiched voraciously. "Kurahashi is a parodist and as such concerns herself with the elaborate use of rhetoric and the imaginative manipulation of established compositional forms" (Sakaki 1995, 392).

The present volume includes eleven stories by Kurahashi Yumiko, drawn from different stages of her career (see the list of the original texts and publication information at the end of the book). I have selected the stories here partly in search of diversity with regard to theme, degree of allusion, and style. Some interesting works have not made the list simply because they are sequels of other stories, or are what I might call "satellite stories"—variations on other works or presentations of other dimensions of the lives of characters' introduced in those works—and thus would not make much sense out of context. I have chosen those that can be read as autonomous texts, although certain of their characters and motifs may resonate with other stories.

The first three stories have in common "supernatural" or "abnormal" beings, acts or phenomena that cannot be accounted for, or accepted, by commonplace logic or the norms of the conventional world. The "supernatural" existence of an extraterrestrial, forbidden acts of incest and bisexual sex, as well as the taboo of hermaphroditism in "An Extraterrestrial," challenge the authenticity of the juridical and medical norms of rationalism, anthropocentricism, exogamy, heterosexuality, and gender as inherent, sustaining, and consistent essences. Kurahashi "uses both incest and sadomasochistic sex to challenge the binary nature of self and other, deconstructing the presupposition of unitary, bounded selfhood." (Orbaugh 128).

The predominant inclination to bestiality in "We Are Lovers," along with the fact that the narrator is a cat, blurs the boundaries between human and nonhuman and again challenges anthropocentricism. "The House of the Black Cat"—which I place after "We Are Lovers," ignoring the respective dates of publication in order to create a hypothetical sequence—presents the transformation of a cat into a female figure, which (who?) has sex with a man. The motifs of metamorphosis and bestiality again blur the distinction between the human and animal worlds and suggest the contingency of scientific taxonomy.

The next three stories are heavily indebted to classical sources, though their relations to their "origins" are not linear but twisted. "The Woman with the Flying Head," as the story's characters note themselves, owes its central motif—the flying head—to *Soushen ji*, or *The Account of Seeking Spirits,* a collection of fantastic stories from the Six Dynasties period of Chinese history, while the pseudo-incest between Genji and Murasaki, and later, Tamakazura, in *Genji monogatari* (*The Tale of Genji*) finds echoes in the character K's relationship with his adopted daughter Li. The neoclassicist appearance notwithstanding, the Kurahashi story dissects the integrity of human anatomy and focuses on the divide between the mind and the body. Which should claim control over the other, when it comes to the identity of the person, and of her child? Anatomically, the child must have been fathered by the man who slept with the woman's body, and as far as the reproductive function of the woman is considered essential, she must be identified as the mother of K's daughter. But while her memory tells her she has had an affair with another man in her dream, it does not tell her anything that has happened to her body while it was without consciousness. Thus, existentially speaking, she is the lover of the man who has never slept with her, and her child is raised, as she should be, by her nonbiological and yet "metaphysically real" father in the end.

"The Trade" draws on two Chinese stories: Tao Qian's "Taohua yuan ji" ("Account of Peach Blossom Spring"), and "Yuming lu" ("Records of the Alive and the Deceased.") Appropriately, the Kurahashi story presents a traffic between dreams and reality, and between fiction and reality—or what is believed to be reality. Within a multilayered narration, the reader is somehow lost in a labyrinth of *déjà lu*. The central theme of the story, however, is the usurpation of the order of importance in self-identification—involving the surface (appearance) and the essence (mind)—and how crucial the former is in the formation of one's self-consciousness and sense of identity. The characters' obsession with their looks—and they are men, who, conventionally, tend to observe female vanity with detachment—reminds us of Noh theater—or any mask theater, for that matter—in which the masks define the roles to be performed. The mask in the title gives an entirely new identity to the one who wears it, drawing her or him from the mediocrity of the ordinary world and into excesses of pleasure and agony, hallucination and death. Sharing the nature of performance, the dance the mask wearer dances not only transforms the performer, but the spectator as well.

"Spring Night Dreams" and "The Passage of Dreams" are perhaps the most traditional of the works collected here, in that they are explicitly and straightforwardly indebted to classical Japanese court literature. While "Spring Night Dreams" cites two poems by Fujiwara no Teika, its primary debt is embodied in its two central characters, who are clearly incarnations of Lady Rokujō and Genji from *The Tale of Genji*—the former, here an assistant professor of literature at a college and a professional novelist, and the latter a statesman whose ambition is to become prime minister. The ancient motif of spirit possession, as well as the transformation of a human being into a demon—a theme the reader will recognize from preceding stories—is employed in this modern-day romance. Yet another example of communication with the dead occurs in "The Passage of Dreams," with its allusion to visits to the realm of dreams found in classical poetry.

"A Special Place" and "Flower Abstraction" are inspired by paintings: Paul Klee's *Auserwaehlte Staette* [*Selected Place*] and Georgia O'Keeffe's *Flower Abstraction,* respectively. The potentially erotic relationship between Kei and his elder first cousin, Mai, which links the two stories, resembles that between Genji and Lady Rokujō, as more directly implied in other stories in the anthology from which the two are taken. While "A Special Place" features a version of Rip Van Winkle's journey through time, or a visit to an unknown place, "Flower Abstraction" presents a blend of high technology and ever unchanging eroticism: "polygamous" relationships via computer communication, and pornographic pictures sent electronically and translated by a scanner.

The last and longest story, "The Long Passage of Dreams," is a composite of seemingly opposing qualities that Kurahashi has demonstrated in separate groups of stories: neoclassicism (allusions to Noh plays and other classical works in the Japanese and Greek literary traditions) versus experimentalism (absurdist incidents occurring out of chronological or causal order); realism (both the author and the female protagonist of this story are the daughters of dentists, and each has a younger brother and sister) versus fantasy (incestuous obsessions, metamorphoses, visits to the realm of the dead); rationalism versus illusion. Such binary oppositions are made and unmade as the story, told at times from the female protagonist's viewpoint and at times from her father's, unfolds. The daughter herself fluctuates between an emotional alliance with her imaginative father and respect for her rational mother. It seems as if the daughter finally makes a decision to live as her mother does, while mourning her father's death. This seems in keeping with Kurahashi's change from absurdist literature to a more logical type of literature, described above. In that sense, the story is autobiographical—not so much because the author's real-life experience is mimetically represented but because Kurahashi's development as a writer is manifested here. Indeed, Kurahashi's fiction is her literary criticism as well. While succeeding in entertaining the reader with her storytelling, Kurahashi also feeds us things to think about—regarding how to write, and what to write.

Works Consulted

Aoyama, Tomoko. "The Love That Poisons: Japanese Parody and the New Literacy." *Japan Forum* 6, no. 1 (April 1994): 35–46.

Keene, Dennis. Introduction to "To Die at the Estuary," ed. Howard Hibbett. *Contemporary Japanese Literature: An Anthology of Fiction, Film, and Other Writing Since 1945*. New York: Knopf, 1977. 247–81.

Kleeman, Faye Yuan. "Sexual Politics and Sexual Poetics in Kurahashi Yumiko's *Cruel Fairy Tales for Adults*. In *Constructions and Confron-*

tations: Changing Representations of Women and Feminism, East and West. Vol. 12 of *Literary Studies, East and West,* ed. Cornelia N. Moore, et al. Honolulu: University of Hawaii, 1996. 150–58.

Lyons, Phyllis. "Women's Narratives and Anti-narratives: Re-reading Japanese Traditions." In *Katachi ∪ Symmetry,* T. Ogawa, et al. Tokyo and New York: Springer, 1996. 109–16.

Napier, Susan J. "The Woman Lost: The Dead, Damaged, or Absent Female in Postwar Fantasy." In *The Fantastic in Modern Japanese Literature: The Subversion of Modernity.* London: Routledge, 1995. 53–92.

Orbaugh, Sharalyn. "The Body in Contemporary Japanese Women's Fiction." In *The Woman's Hand: Gender and Theory in Japanese Women's Writing,* ed. Paul Gordon Schalow and Janet A. Walker. Stanford: Stanford University Press, 1996. 119–64.

Sakaki, Atsuko. "Denaturalizing Nature, Dissolving the Self: An Analysis of Kurahashi Yumiko's *Popoi.*" In *Nature and Selfhood in Japanese Literature,* ed. Kinya Tsuruta. Vancouver, B.C.: Josai University and the University of British Columbia, 1993. 241–56.

———. "Fiddling with Daddy's Tune: Kurahashi Yumiko's Parody of the Fathers." In *Because Woman Spoke First,* ed. Esperanza Ramirez-Christensen and Rebecca Copeland. Work in progress.

———. "A Gallery of 'Severed Heads': A Comparative Study of Yumiko Kurahashi's *Popoi.*" In *Dramas of Desire/Visions of Beauty,* ed. Ziva Ben-Porat et al. Vol. 1 of *The Force of Vision,* ed. Earl Miner and Toru Haga. 386–93.

———. "The Intertextual Novel and the Interrelational Self: Kurahashi Yumiko, A Japanese Postmodernist." Ph.D. diss., University of British Columbia, 1992.

———. "(Re)Canonizing Kurahashi Yumiko in Post-Modern Contexts: Toward Alternative Perspectives in Studies of 'Modern' 'Japanese' 'Literature.' " In *On Beyond Ōe: Contemporary Japanese Fiction,* ed. Stephen Snyder and Philip Gabriel. Work in progress.

Vernon, Victoria V. *Daughters of the Moon: Wish, Will and Social Constraint in Fiction by Modern Japanese Women.* Berkeley: University of California Press, 1988.

Works of Kurahashi Yumiko Translated into English

The Adventures of Sumiyakist Q [Sumiyakisuto Kyū no bōken, 1969]. Trans. Dennis Keene. St. Lucia, Queensland: University of Queensland Press, 1979.

Divine Maiden [*Seishōjo,* 1965]. Trans. Bertha Lynn Burson. [Translation of part 1 of *Seishōjo*] "Divine Maiden: Kurahashi Yumiko's *Seishōjo.*" Ph.D. diss., University of Texas at Austin, 1989. 1–66.

"The Boy Who Became an Eagle" [Washi ni natta shōnen, 1961]. Trans. Samuel Grolmes and Yumiko Tsumura. *New Directions in Prose and Poetry* 29 (1974): 116–33.

"The End of Summer" [Natsu no owari, 1960]. Trans. Victoria V. Vernon. In *Daughters of the Moon: Wish, Will and Social Constraint in Fiction by Modern Japanese Women.* Berkeley: University of California, 1988. 229–40.

"The Little Girl with the Silver Hair" [Shiroi kami no dōjo, 1969]. Trans. Kumiko Nakanishi. "The Life and Works of Yumiko Kurahashi." Master's thesis, San Diego State University, 1987.

"The Monastery" [Kyosatsu, 1961]. Trans. Carolyn Haynes. In *The Shōwa Anthology: Modern Japanese Short Stories Vol. 2: 1961–1984,* ed. Van C. Gessel and Tomone Matsumoto. Tokyo: Kōdansha, 1985. 218–31.

"Partei" [Parutai, 1960]. Trans. Samuel Grolmes and Yumiko Tsumura. *New Directions in Prose and Poetry* 26 (1973): 8–22.

[Parutai.] Trans. Yukiko Tanaka and Elizabeth Hanson. *This Kind of Woman: Ten Stories by Japanese Women Writers 1960–1976.* New York: Putnam, 1982. 1–16.

"To Die at the Estuary" [Kakō ni shisu, 1970]. Trans. Denis Keene. In *Contemporary Japanese Literature: An Anthology of Fiction, Film, and Other Writing Since 1945,* ed. Howard Hibbett. New York: Knopf, 1977. 248–81.

"The Ugly Devils" [Shūma tachi, 1965]. Trans. Samuel Grolmes and Yumiko Tsumura. *New Directions in Prose and Poetry* 24 (1972): 55–67.

"Week for the Extermination of the Mongrels" [Zatsujin bokumetsu shūkan, 1960]. Trans. Samuel Grolmes and Yumiko Tsumura. *Mundus Artium: A Journal of International Literature and the Arts* 14, no. 1 (1983): 103–13.

THE WOMAN WITH THE FLYING HEAD

AND OTHER STORIES
BY KURAHASHI YUMIKO

An Extraterrestrial
(Uchūjin (1964))

When I woke up with my leg dangling over the side of the bed, my foot touched something other than the floor. It was strange that my slippers were not there as usual. But what made me more uneasy still was the odd texture of the thing I now stroked with the sole of my foot. It was like a huge egg. *Egg?* I was ready to scream. It certainly felt like an egg—hard, smooth, yet fragile. It certainly felt like one. I could almost thrust my foot into it up to my thigh with a single forceful step. If it was an egg though, it had to be an unusually big one.

Staring at the ceiling, I debated whether I should get out of bed or not. I was overwhelmed by the fear that when I jumped onto the floor, it might turn out to be the shell of an egg—it might break and swallow me into its depths. I told myself not to be afraid of the egg; it was merely a sequel to some childish dream. So when I actually found a big egg rocking at my feet, I was no longer surprised.

Without doubt, it was an egg, one far bigger than my pillow, that was rolling beside the bed as if I had laid it a moment ago.

"L, someone's laid an egg!" I cried, wondering to myself, But who's done that? I couldn't think of any creature capable of producing such an egg. I crossed the room to wake my elder sister L, who seemed still to be asleep and lay facing the opposite wall.

If you want to wake up L, you've got to trick her like you do a slumbering cat. Certainly she looked the part. She thrust her legs out of the futon like a cat thrusting its claws out of its tender flesh, languidly opening eyes that gleamed with obvious ill-humor.

I was tickling her warm feet when L suddenly stood up like an adolescent soldier awakened by the morning bugle call.

"I just said there was an egg," I offered, a little apologetically. Combing her long hair with the fingers of one hand, L gazed straight at the egg and said without smiling, "It's the egg of an Extraterrestrial."

"An Extraterrestrial?"

"Sure. What else could it be?"

I was smiling vaguely, intimidated by her certainty. I felt as if this sister, only two years older than I, had suddenly become as mature as our mother, leaving me way back in the toy box to peep out by myself into the world of grown-ups. It seemed she must have some knowledge that qualified her as an adult, as there was no excitement or astonishment on her face. This disappointed me even more. I didn't even feel like staying in bed with L as usual, the two of us tickling each other like a pair of cats until Mom started shouting.

"What should we do?" I mumbled, all confidence gone from my voice. I expected L to come up with some excellent idea, as she would usually do when we conspired to hide or break something. Yet she said solemnly, "Of course, we have to hatch it."

"The question is, how," I replied immediately, gazing at L's lips, which were sealed tightly and authoritatively like a schoolteacher's.

"We should keep it warm in the bed."

What a good idea, I thought. I tried to lift the egg onto

my bed. I rolled it upright and pushed it up with L's help. I was all nervous, afraid that I would break it. By the time we were done, I was drenched in sweat.

Every morning after that, we woke up with the expectation that the egg would have hatched, and that an unfamiliar-looking animal would be lying on the floor. However, we found nothing on the clean linoleum. We would peep under the bed from both sides, look at each other's upside-down faces, and then proceed to divest ourselves of both pajamas and thwarted expectations. We would examine the egg only to find no change. I supposed that the animal we awaited must be of a very advanced and complex species, and L agreed with me. "Well, we shouldn't be impatient," L would say in the tone of a nonchalant hen as she pushed her belly against the egg at night. I, in contrast, was very concerned. Perhaps our method of hatching it was fundamentally wrong. Perhaps we should chill this unusual egg rather than keeping it warm. After all, this was an Extraterrestrial's egg, anything that went against our common sense might be right. Nevertheless, L remained self-confident. Removing the blanket and shifting the egg to a sunny place—L suggested that we should warm the egg in the sunshine during the daytime—she tapped the shell with her fingers and, with her ear pressed against it, listened for any sound coming from inside.

"I can't hear anything. It won't hatch very soon."

"How long will it take?"

"A week at least."

It sounded as if the rule of Hartree were applicable to the egg. The invariable of Von Neumann was a week, so that whenever one asked the question, the answer was always "in a week." L looked so serious when she said this that it seemed the egg were truly governed by this joke-like principle.

"There's no need to rush. The egg will definitely hatch."

But I had reached the point where I could not rid myself of the anticipation of something ominous. Perhaps some subversion had happened in the egg a long time ago, and it was already too late to make amends, no matter how long the egg bathed in the sun. For all we knew, the longer it bathed in the sun, mightn't the death inside be growing ever bigger? Mightn't it be a lump of ghastly death and decay that appeared when, unable to wait any longer, we at last broke the shell?

L laughed at my concerns and left home for college. But she was back in a moment; she must have sensed the possibility that I might do something to the egg during her absence. Her intuition was amazingly acute and correct in this case—to be precise, I had decided to break the egg that very day without L's permission. Having equipped myself with a small mountaineer's ax and hammer, I was gazing intently at the egg, wrapped in a downy aura of dreamlike light. L must have seen me as she approached the half-open door from outside. "Stop, don't be so rash!" She sprung into the room breathlessly, as if to stop a suicide attempt, and grabbed me around the belly from behind. Nonetheless, I swung the ax down into the egg, without knowing what the consequence might be.

The shell broke all too easily. Though I had struck it without much force, so as not to harm its contents, it cracked like thin ice. The unspent momentum of the ax carried it deep into the egg, as if it would be swallowed up entirely. L cried out as if she had just reached orgasm. Then the ax really did disappear from my hands into the egg. Why had I let it go? I looked in through the fissure but couldn't see anything.

"What have you done? You must have cut the baby inside!"

L thrust me aside and looked within. "There's nothing."

It was utterly dark inside. Any dark space must reveal something when light shines into it, but this darkness rejected light as a dense substance would. It was not, however, some viscous fluid or solid matter—there was nothing, not even a thin gas. I had an uneasy feeling as I groped around inside it.

"Chicken!" said L. Tucking up her sleeves like a housewife devotedly launching into household chores, she thrust her arm up to the shoulder into the egg. I stared in amazement to discover such brazen boldness in her. Then she turned pale, trying in vain to scream and gesturing me to help her. I thought the animal in the egg must have become upset at L's relentless probing and had bitten her hand as a cornered rat would. I pulled on her arm with all my might, and L fell back helplessly onto her hips. But she hadn't lost her arm: it had neither melted into the darkness inside the egg nor been torn off by the unidentified animal. I was relieved to see it, as slender as ever, suspended just so from her shoulder.

"What happened? Who was inside?"

"No one." L shook her head with an expression of absolute negation. "There was no one—or, nothing, as if it were in space."

I thought it couldn't be just an ordinary, empty space. It must be different from a petty vacuum. I looked into it again, feeling mesmerized, as if catching a glimpse of another universe. For no particular reason I felt like disappearing through the dark hole into somewhere else. The temptation was so great it made me tremble. L must have felt the same thing. We mustn't grope around so haphazardly anymore. Such was the position L, recovering the dignity proper to an older sister, now adopted. Treating me all too blatantly like a child, she looked determined not to let an innocent boy be seduced into such a thing.

"Seeing it has turned out this way," L stated, sounding like the foreman at a construction site, "all we can do is smash it up."

Smash what?—but I didn't have time to question L. She fetched the small hammer and began single-mindedly beating at the egg. The shell cracked easily, breaking into fragments, which fell into the darkness they had enclosed, disappearing with every stroke of the hammer.

"Don't get too close!" Saying this, L destroyed about a third of the shell in a twinkling. The egg-shaped darkness, now deprived of its skin, revealed its exposed head. How ridiculous! Darkness was supposed to disappear, eroded by the light. Instead, this darkness stuck part of itself out into the light, still retaining the shape of the egg, the rest still covered with its white shell—the protruding part looked like the smooth and glossy penis. Associating its spectacle with I didn't know what, L began to laugh raucously, without stopping, as if she had gone mad.

But then our joyous laughter died. I swallowed my breath, and L's voice froze with the tears still welling in her eyes. Out of the egg—or more precisely, out of the egg-shaped darkness, an Extraterrestrial appeared.

I don't know how I identified it as an Extraterrestrial, but I had no doubt about its being one. It crawled out on its hands and knees, innocently, without malice or embarrassment. There was no darkness anymore. It must have closed off behind the Extraterrestrial, the way an exit or entrance would. Though we had witnessed the whole incident, the situation appeared too ambiguous to explain exactly what had happened and how. At any rate the Extraterrestrial was there, in the posture of a baby who had just learned how to crawl. It seemed not to have come from another world but to have existed there forever in just this posture—naked, with some fragments of shell still clinging to it. It might have taken us quite a long time to notice that the Extraterrestrial was naked. One would never expect any baby, of any animal whatsoever, to be born clothed. In addition the Extraterrestrial had no hair at all, not even on its head, which may have strengthened the impact of its nakedness. It's not that I had expected some hairy animal like a monkey, but I hadn't expected the animal that hatched to be so mannequin-like. I found it somehow funny, and I grinned unrestrainedly. L glared at me with reproachful eyes, as if she were looking at a child molester. She must have misunderstood my intention. Realizing I should be ashamed of myself for showing an undue interest in the naked Extraterrestrial, I laughed to hide my embarrassment and said, "It's about time for Dad to come back. We should tie the Extraterrestrial to one of the bedposts before he does."

L disagreed furiously—that would be too impolite, she said. And when she had said so, it seemed to me that she might be right. I didn't know why. In short, I didn't know what to do with the Extraterrestrial.

"Now we must help it take a bath," said L. She sounded like a young wife, with me as her young husband. A young couple who had just had their first baby. We decided to take the Extraterrestrial to the bathroom. I took its hand. It felt much the same as my sister's hand, which made me feel a little funny. But I told myself that what was most important for now was not to let it go, and I tried to drag it into the bathroom forcibly. I took for granted that it wouldn't like taking a bath, just like a dog, and I did feel it resisting, so I pulled its hand with all my might. But then the Extraterrestrial had a bad fall, perhaps slipping on the wet floor.

"Watch out!" cried L, and lifted its head onto her lap. I looked anxiously into its face, but it had no expression. We couldn't know how it felt, for it was without eyes or mouth. It wasn't that the face had no features; it was humanly shaped, except that the eyes and mouth were just dark holes, like the darkness inside the egg. It would look more natural with artificial eyeballs and teeth, I thought. Such holes made a person feel uneasy.

L was absorbed in washing the Extraterrestrial's body. She started with its arms, then proceeded to its neck, and then lathered its breasts generously. They were shaped like a woman's—the Extraterrestrial must be female. How could I have overlooked it till then? I was about to mention this to L when I saw her pear-shaped breasts dangling under her slip as she bent over the Extraterrestrial. I absently compared her breasts with the Extraterrestrial's; while tiny nipples stuck out of L's breasts, the Extraterrestrial's looked more like the rear ends of apples. It appeared that holes gaped into the darkness there too. Its navel also looked like a deep hole. When I craned my neck to look more closely, L's contemptuous eyes froze me.

Hastily lathering my hands, I said, "Shall I help you?"

L snorted, and declared coldly, "No, thank you. Boys needn't look."

My body became hot with embarrassment, and yet I felt my curiosity hardened and swollen somewhere in my body. Troubled by this awareness, I secretly watched L's hands making their way between the Extraterrestrial's thighs. All of sudden, L stood up. She looked not surprised but indignant.

"What's up?"

"Don't ask. You just wash it."

I discovered in the soap lather below its belly an erect rosy pillar. It appeared to be a lethal weapon, which had just hurt L's hand. It must be the same thing that I had. But why did it stand upright, shining brilliantly, like my own shame? I couldn't breathe. L burst into laughter, rolling back her tongue, at the utterly comic nature of the situation. I couldn't even laugh anymore.

When she stopped laughing, L said to it in a maternal tone, "Now stand up straight. Be good." And she resumed washing its male part and its legs, without any hesitation, as if washing a pillar. I gazed intently at the mysterious pillar projecting from its front. The swelling of the breasts was obviously female, while the surplus in the crotch was male. Despite this unusual figure, the Extraterrestrial didn't look grotesque at all. Rather, it seemed to me that androgyny must be an appropriate attribute for an Extraterrestrial. An idea occurred to me: perfect humans. This ethyl ether-like volatile notion made me giddy.

"Here, look at this," called L, enthusiastically. She grasped the Extraterrestrial's ankles and pulled its legs up, as if it were a baby having its diaper changed. Of course it was not as small as a baby, so that the indecency of the sight shocked me deeply. L called me closer, saying, "Look," and waving with one hand.

I drew closer, faking a sort of enthusiasm. We observed it like medical students in anatomy class. The tension and excitement made me feel as if I were wearing glittering contact lenses. At first, that part of the Extraterrestrial looked extremely complex. I was very conscious that it was beyond my comprehension, and my eyes were veiled behind an opaque membrane of embarrassment, which made me even more confused. I mumbled, "It doesn't have hair here, either."

"Don't be silly." L pinched me on the side. "Look closely, and open your eyes properly."

"It looks grotesque," I said unconsciously.

This immediately displeased L. Saying, "Sort of," she

stood up. I felt a little more at ease to observe it then. It still looked complicated and grotesque, and as if ready to bite me. This must be because I was not used to the sight, I thought. But one never gets used to looking at some things, no matter how often one may look at them—such as female genitals. And in fact, what I was looking at with my own eyes could be nothing else but female genitals. But I wasn't certain; I had never seen any. Perhaps the Extraterrestrial's genitals were disfigured. I looked up at L's face.

"What do you think?" asked L.

"Is yours like this, too?" I asked.

"Don't be silly. What have you been looking at?"

"I mean," I corrected myself, like a student who has failed an oral exam, "the female part is shaped like this, right?"

"Oh, that," L mumbled, "probably, yes."

"Don't you know for sure? You have it yourself," I went on, puffed up.

"Because," L said uncertainly, "I can't see it myself."

"That's no good. You have to know. You are getting married next month."

"So what?"

L tried to attack me, whirling the towel. This was not unusual, but we should have known better than to wrestle with each other at this point. I said to her calmly, "Let's not quarrel now," and looked at her with innocent and tender eyes, the way one might cajole a cat. L was mollified, as if she had met the eyes of a faithful dog; she felt good, thinking she was loved. She was not wrong—I loved her in a sense.

Returning to practical matters, L opened her arms and swept up the Extraterrestrial with a theatrical flourish.

"Let's finish washing it quickly, before Mom or Dad comes home."

I agreed. I didn't know how we'd explain the situation to them if they caught sight of us. We hadn't even told them about the egg. But now that the Extraterrestrial, as big as the average of me and L, had been born from the egg, we wouldn't be able to keep it a secret very long. We could count on Mom's experience in raising kids, and we would need Dad to approve of the budget for feeding it and other costs.

"But we had better not tell them about that," I said.

L looked at me with a witch-like eye, through disheveled hair. It looked like a third eye that had been asleep in the middle of her brow. When I pointed to the part with both male and female genitals, she nodded, and said as if casting a spell, "Oh, Hermaphrodite!"

"Is anyone home?" It was Mom—how could she be back so early? Had she canceled her evening class? (She was an associate professor of comparative literature at the university I was enrolled in.) L quickly slid home the latch on the bathroom door and answered, "I'm helping the Extraterrestrial take a bath."

"You mustn't mention the Extraterrestrial, we'll be in trouble," I whispered. But Mom had already responded in the sturdy, high-pressured voice in which she gave lectures, "Is K there, too?"

"Yes, it takes the two of us. It is quite big."

What an absurd answer!

"I beg your pardon?"

"It's the ET she's talking about!" I shouted desperately. Mom was silent for a few seconds—she must have been imagining how an ET would look.

"I hope it's not violent," she ventured at last.

"It's very meek," L replied. After wrapping the Extraterrestrial's trunk in a bath towel, she opened the door for Mom. "Here you go, Mom."

"My, my," Mom said casually. "It's going to catch a cold with just a towel on. Let it wear your robe, L." Putting on an apron, she disappeared into the kitchen.

I looked at L in disappointment. L shrugged her shoulders at me. Perhaps grown-ups of Mom's age did not find extraterrestrials particularly exotic. Still, she could at least have tried to take a look at it. Her eyes looked exactly like those of a beheaded hen. When she saw anything amoral or absurd, her eyes took on that look. That is why I sometimes almost feel like slaughtering women over forty years old.

I went into the kitchen, feeling I needed to explain the situation further. Mom was dicing a piece of chicken thigh, with her back to me. This left me unable to speak.

"Tell L to come," said Mom, "she should help me with cooking at least tonight—Mr. S is coming to dinner, you know."

S is L's fiancé, and a lecturer in economic history.

In a short while Dad came home too. (He was a prosecutor.) I told him about the Extraterrestrial, which caused him to look grim. "How could such a thing have got into our house?" he said suspiciously. "Someone must have been keeping it as a pet. Wild extraterrestrials can't possibly show up in the middle of the city."

"Actually, it was born out of an egg in our bedroom. The egg was this big."

"So enormous? In that case I suppose the shell is still around?"

"Well, the shell was all lost in a hole. I don't know how to explain it to you, but the shell disappeared into the infinite darkness, so to speak, that the shell used to enclose."

"How could any citizen believe you?" Dad snapped in his prosecutor's voice. "Not a shred of evidence remains. Anyway, you'll have to report it to the police as lost property; it must have come from somebody's home. If its owner remains unidentified and we keep it, we will have to have it registered at the public health office."

"I'm afraid the ET is not that kind of animal. Couldn't you take a look at it?"

"Wait. Let me take a bath first."

Wondering how both Mom and Dad could be so unconcerned, I went into the dining room. There L sat the Extraterrestrial down at the table to drink some milk. The doorbell rang.

"It must be S. What shall we do with the Extraterrestrial?"

"No problem. We should just introduce it to everyone."

That made sense, I thought. However, like Mom and Dad, S showed hardly any interest in the Extraterrestrial. They were too busy enthusiastically exchanging greetings to look at it, or to let us introduce them to it.

Engaged men appear somewhat comical. They make their heads and shoes shine, wear formal clothes, and walk around with the price tags on their backs. L's fiancé was no exception to the general rule. Moreover, he looked like a pig lost on a university campus—he was too fat for a thirty-year-old man. I told L so all the time, and she agreed with me, saying nevertheless that she would prefer such a man as a husband. L, too, pretended to be an ordinary girl who went to church on Sundays and giggled even at such trivial things as when she dropped a fork on a plate. She was just acting out a farce. L was like a cat, who looked far more attractive when not smiling.

S began to eat vehemently, snorting when the dinner was ready. He seemed out of breath when he ate because he was overweight, which made him seem all the more like a pig. I tried in vain to convey this message to L, but she was absorbed in feeding the Extraterrestrial, who lay at her feet.

"It's a very obedient Extraterrestrial," S offered by way of a compliment. It sounded as though a dog had praised a cat, which upset me.

"It's not an ordinary Extraterrestrial. It's androgynous."

"Androgynous? It's disfigured, then."

"You mean a hermaphrodite? I've seen one in a photograph in a book of medical law," Dad cut in. "Doesn't the word come from Hermes and Aphrodite in Greek mythology?"

"Yes, it does," Mom replied with a grim face, which told us not to touch upon sexual issues. The next moment Mom said to S cordially, not as an associate professor of comparative literature but as a housewife, "How about another piece of fried chicken, Mr. S?"

"Please let the Extraterrestrial have one too," said L. She had lifted the Extraterrestrial onto her lap.

"Oh, L, watch your manners!"

Ignoring Mom's reproach, she rapidly thrust the food into the Extraterrestrial's mouth.

"Look, it eats a lot," said L, impressed. I however heard a distant sign of danger humming in my head—perhaps the Extraterrestrial might eat as much as it pleased. I remembered the uncanny darkness inside the egg. If the Extraterrestrial enclosed a dark space of the same kind inside itself, we could throw anything into its mouth, and as much as we wanted. It might sound absurd, but perhaps the Extraterrestrial could eat infinitely—perhaps it could swallow everything in the world.

"What a big appetite! That's good; it looks energetic and healthy," said S, and tried to feed the Extraterrestrial a piece of fried chicken from his plate. The next moment, its mouth gaped with the abruptness of a marionette's, and S's wrist was gone—hidden in the mouth of the Extraterrestrial, that is. Had the mouth attacked the hand, or was the hand drawn into it? Among the screaming voices I grinned, and L winked at me. I was convinced that L must have incited it to swallow S's hand. S went pale and looked like a certain thing made of thin rubber, shrinking rapidly.

"Behave yourself, my dear," said L in a singsong voice, and drew S's hand back out into the air. He contemplated it as if it had been produced from an alligator's mouth, almost wondering how it could remain part of his body.

"You are such a chicken," laughed L. I was heartily satisfied.

"It must be done away with at the health center if it does harm to human beings and pets!" screamed Dad. "Perhaps we'd better take it to the police and have it temporarily placed in custody. In any case, we shouldn't keep it without official permission."

In anger, L threw the fork in her hand into the Extraterrestrial's mouth. We were all taken aback. I thought I heard a dull clang, as if the fork had been thrown into a mailbox. That's not right. Actually it disappeared without any sound at all. Where could it have gone?

"Do away with it now, quickly!" said Mom.

"Don't be silly. You would be punished for malicious abandonment of a dangerous object and for violating the Road Traffic Act."

"How dare you suggest that I abandon it!" said L in a terrifying fury, standing up with the Extraterrestrial and putting her arm through its.

"Where are you going?"

"For a walk."

"Then you should go with Mr. S," said Dad. But L left the dining room, saying "I am going with the Extraterrestrial." I don't think she had ever behaved this way in S's presence.

"We are so sorry. She is such a temperamental girl," said Mom. "I hope you are not hurt."

"I think I'm okay," said S awkwardly. "I wasn't bitten by it." S rubbed his arm as if to rub off the traces of the void that had touched his skin. "Yet I think it is dangerous."

I went out of the house in pursuit of L and the Extraterrestrial. As I had expected, L had been stopped at the police stand at the corner of the main street. The middle-level police officer who was interrogating L stood upright, hardly even glancing at the Extraterrestrial.

"You have to keep it on a chain. Besides, it appears that it hasn't been registered yet."

"Where can I have it registered?"

"At the public health center. Has it had its shot?"

"You mean for rabies?"

"Yes. Moreover, it should not go around naked. Cover its hips with a cloth or something. As its owner, you have to take responsibility for its excretions."

He sounded like Dad. We laughed about it afterward.

Dad went on a long business trip the following day. Mom was busy in her office at the university. So we did not have to chain it or register it but rather began living with the naked Extraterrestrial.

Within a week, however, we were almost fed up with the Extraterrestrial. It wasn't that it troubled us by peeing everywhere, being infected with syphilis, or detesting human beings—there was no trouble of that kind. For example, we did not have to worry about its excretions. We had planned to get a litter-box, the kind you use for kittens, until the Extraterrestrial grew up and learned how to use the bathroom. But then we discovered that it never excreted anything, no matter how much it had eaten. Moreover—we should have realized this earlier—we didn't have to feed the Extraterrestrial in the first place. If we wanted, it would have eaten a whole cow or truck. But it would have been like throwing things into a bottomless abyss; a torrent of things would disappear without trace into the confined space within its body. We tried throwing all kinds of things into its mouth when we were bored—a game that soon lost its appeal.

If the Extraterrestrial had had a voracious appetite we would have panicked, fearing that we would soon be eaten up. Fortunately, however, the Extraterrestrial made no demands. It was entirely obedient. This was only natural, for it wanted nothing and didn't care about losing anything. We could manipulate its body as we liked. Perhaps one could put it this way: we must have manipulated the Extraterrestrial's body by directing its consciousness or spirit, if it had anything like that. But I don't know if it did have consciousness or a spirit. If one could define a dog's consciousness as some movement of its psyche that makes it wag its tail, then the Extraterrestrial did not have consciousness; it never depended upon its masters. In this regard, its obedience was more like a doll's than a pet's. For this reason, we felt somewhat at a loss. The Extraterrestrial moved as we wanted it to. Thus, we got into the habit of always wanting it to do something.

But we became tired of wanting it to do something. Once we kicked it into a corner of our room and left it there for a few days. It lay there in the same posture, looking not like a broken doll but like some lazy, arrogant bum. It became so dusty I dragged it up and dusted it off. I kept dusting it until I began to practice boxing with the Extraterrestrial as if it were a punching bag. I quickly stopped, though; it was spooky when my fists sank into its flesh—it felt as if there was nothing behind it.

Several days later L went to a department store and

bought a wig somewhat lighter in color than her own hair, to put on the Extraterrestrial's head. That wig of curly hair made it look like a store mannequin. The face, by contrast, looked like that of a Greek sculpture—a masculine Aphrodite. Probably this was because it didn't have eyeballs.

L had the Extraterrestrial sit in front of the dressing table, and began to style its hair as carefully as a meticulous professional beautician would. Before long L began to enjoy this. Once its hair was done, she would make it up. L became enthusiastic about dressing and undressing the Extraterrestrial, taking out all the clothes she had. Sometimes she would go out shopping with the Extraterrestrial and come back with sweaters, blouses, necklaces, and bracelets to share with it. "Let it wear your shirts and sweaters," L said. Indeed, the Extraterrestrial looked fine in men's attire, as long as its breasts were properly concealed.

L thus made the Extraterrestrial into her mannequin. She started saying, "I'll play with the Extraterrestrial," which somehow annoyed me; she said it as if she were using the phrase *play with* in the sense of playing with a doll, rather than with a friend or a dog or cat. L seemed to think of the Extraterrestrial not as a dog or cat, but as a doll. It was beyond my comprehension that L, who had never played with dolls since she was small, should have become absorbed with a "doll" at the age of twenty. And above all, I could not bear L's sleeping with the Extraterrestrial dressed in a negligee.

It was on a languid Saturday afternoon in April that I did it for the first time. The others—Dad, Mom, even L—were not at home—it must have been when they were having the final discussions about the wedding with S's family over lunch. Around the same time, I had been devastated when I kissed my girlfriend—whom my parents had acknowledged as such—for the first time, desired to do something more, and was promptly rejected. I swear that it was she who first penetrated my lips with her tongue. This encouraged me to proceed, until I heard those words buzzing like a horsefly around my ears: *not now* and *marriage.* I drew back, to find the girl looking at me challengingly. Her face looked exactly like that of my forty-year-old mother. On top of that, she said, "You're such a child." I should have bitten off her tongue when it was in my mouth.

I came home with the warm sap still oozing from the scar of my broken desire. I began to console myself in the way any boy knows—still imagining her face, frustratingly enough. The Extraterrestrial was lying in L's bed, wrapped in a blanket. I didn't like being watched by it. I tried in vain to persuade myself that it wouldn't matter, that it was something like a doll. The problem was the eyeballs. The cheap artificial eyes L had stuck in its face were looking at me. Those eyes made its face look like that of a virginal angel. Still, they were fake. I poked them out with my cruel fingers. In their place appeared two black holes, from which the scent of nothingness rose like a dark flame. The angel's face was transformed into that of a devil—my own face. I kissed it on its opened lips. It was no secular kiss, with teeth clicking, the tongue penetrating, and saliva flowing back and forth. I was directly kissing the nothingness that was about to draw me in. I extended my tongue and let it swim freely in the other world. I realized that somehow his penis was in my hands, and mine in his, and that we had been making love like two men. Then, we made love like a man and woman. A piece of cellophane tape had been applied to the Extraterrestrial's vagina—the part of its body that came from Aphrodite. L must have done that.

When I came back to my senses, L was standing there,

looking down at us. She stopped talking to me after that night, and the Extraterrestrial came to belong to me, sleeping in my bed.

It was no trouble at all for L to get it back. It was my turn, one day, to witness L having sex with the Extraterrestrial. I realized in the juicy morning light that my arms were empty—and that the slender form of L was riding a horse at an infinitely rapid pace.

Eventually L and I came to put our two beds next to each other, and we would sleep with the Extraterrestrial between us, holding it from either side. We looked over its shoulders into each other's eyes, sharing it; I used its feminine part, L the masculine. Between me and L lay the nothingness enclosed by the fake flesh, our universe, so to speak. This chunk of nothingness was shaped like a hermaphrodite—the perfect human being, that is. We must have craved to enter it to achieve a perfect existence. But the guileful L betrayed me, planning to live on like a spider, taking advantage of Dad, Mom, S, and the network of society. When I thought about this, I couldn't resist anymore. I lost control of myself and tried to hug L along with the Extraterrestrial. But it was impossible to squeeze the infinite darkness inside the Extraterrestrial. I pushed it away, and assaulted L directly—to no avail. How could I utter the words, "I love you, L!" The next moment reality showed its claws, leaving us full of scars.

"What are you going to do with the Extraterrestrial when I am married?" asked L.

"You can take it if you like." I didn't care anymore.

It was so muggy that morning that I couldn't wake up. Though I felt I no longer slept, dreams stuck between my eyelids, like yellow glue, and powerlessness filled my mind like grains of sand. Was it because I'd done it again with the Extraterrestrial? As the sand leaked out of my ears little by little, I noticed it had somehow grown noisy in the house: the ringing of bells, overlapping conversations, loud footsteps. Through the din there sounded from time to time trumpet peals of festivity. A lot of cars seemed to be parked out front. Quite a few people had arrived already. With this thought, I willfully kept my eyes shut. Then I remembered it was L's wedding day. They had come to meet L, I thought vaguely. However, strangely, I could hear Mom screaming from the third floor, "Please don't mess the room up so!" It sounded as if there was some trouble regarding the removal of L.

"I have already explained to you twice," a man said. He sounded rather irritated, frustrated with Mom's response. I heard such words as "disposal," "contract," and "removal" uttered loudly by Mom. Did it mean that the zoo had sent some people to take the Extraterrestrial into custody? Or judging from their serious tone, perhaps we were being subjected to a household search on suspicion that we had kept the Extraterrestrial illegally. I held it tight in bed, determined not to let them take it. If I pretended to be indulging in sex, the police officers would look away and say, "Oh, excuse me." No, that's a ridiculous idea, I thought, still holding the Extraterrestrial in my arms. Then, its "thing" became hard, as did mine, and got in my way. Nevertheless, I, as a man, made love to it, as a woman, inserting myself into its female part. I felt as if my blood and flesh were being sucked into another world. I would die if I kept on, I told myself with a quiver. But I couldn't stop myself. The thought occurred to me that I wouldn't care no matter what happened to me.

However, it seemed I had to be present in the "disposal" and "removal" of L. I descended to the parlor downstairs, where I discovered something like a coffin. Folded up in it was L, looking very cramped. Mom was asking some tedious questions. A go-between in black was responding to her in a fine, shrill, womanish voice. He sounded as if he were expressing sympathy. It was then that custodians, who looked like black ogres, covered L's body with a coarse cloth. "Will you come to watch it as it happens there?" asked the go-between. Dad said in a dignified manner, "No." Mom was sobbing, as if to squeeze out tears. The custodians lifted the box with L inside. I didn't know what to do. Beside myself, I cried, "Come running back soon! I will be waiting for you, taking proper care of the Extraterrestrial!"

"Wake up, son." I heard Dad say. "L's wedding is scheduled for noon. You were supposed to get up earlier and go along with L and Mom. Your mother and the others have gone to the hotel, you know."

"I see." I got up and asked anxiously, "What happened to the Extraterrestrial?"

"I don't know anything about it," said Dad, standing there like a pyramid inscribed with THE PROSECUTOR on the desk in court. He sounded as if he had steeled his will in the matter.

"Has L taken it with her? I hope you didn't have it put into police custody or taken to the zoo without our knowing?"

"You've got no right to interrogate me." Saying this, Dad tensed the muscles in his face as if to remind me that he was a prosecutor rather than my father. "Why are you so attached to that thing? You're not a child anymore—and neither is L. It's all right to keep Extraterrestrials as pets, but not to the extent that they ruin your normal lives. L's life as a married woman begins today. After she's established a respectable household and she's raised her children properly, then she can keep an Extraterrestrial as a hobby. By then, Extraterrestrials will be common and recognized as sound pets."

My eyes became inflamed with a shame akin to anger. I couldn't listen to my father. I tried to make a retort but couldn't say anything, realizing that he was still taller, with a knife-like nose and glittering eyeglasses.

He said tenderly, "Hurry up and get ready now. I've tied up the Extraterrestrial and put it in the attic. We'll talk about what to do with it after we come home."

There were a lot of people at the wedding banquet by the time we arrived. On both sides of tables as long as rivers—and there were quite a few of them—people in black were lined up. The overall effect was of hundreds of crows thronging the ground. I wanted to say a word of farewell to L but didn't have the chance to—I'd come late, and L and S were already seated up front. Mom and Dad, with S's parents, seemed to be sitting on either side of them. My seat was so far away that I couldn't even make out L's expression. It seemed to me, however, that her eyes were downcast, while S looked around at the guests with a smile on his greasy face. When the organ sounded loudly, bride and groom cut the wedding cake with joined hands, and guest after guest stood up to make a speech. L must have been afraid that she might burst into raucous laughter like a madwoman if she ever looked up—especially if she were to make eye contact with me. Indeed, the proceedings as a whole were quite ridiculous. How could L repress today that insidious impulse that usually boils over as imprudent laughter?

But these people looked serious, even sorrowful. A number of former classmates of L's and S's talked about funny blunders both of them had made and kept secret, but no one except the speaker even laughed. These grown-ups grew more and more taciturn, their expressions grave. They were waiting for the speeches to end so that they could let loose the flood of eating. After a while, guests began grimly conferring with one another in undertones. "Excuse me, are you an acquaintance of the bride?" asked the gentleman next to me. "Yes," I replied, and ate a fried prawn. Before I'd swallowed it, I heard more hand clapping, and my name called by the organizer. He asked me, as the brother of the bride, to make a speech. At a loss as to what to do, I wished for the floor to gape open and swallow me up. Instead, my body soared like a high tower on my legs. I loved L as I would love a noble cat, but I thought it would be out of place to say that. Nonetheless, I realized I had begun talking about something even more out of place—the Extraterrestrial. All at once I was eloquent beyond control, as I explained how marvelous this Extraterrestrial was that L and I owned. I told them that it had in its body a sheer dark void like the universe, and that it could eat infinitely, without ever excreting. As I spoke, I became gay and began to laugh. But no one else did. They were all wistfully eyeing emptied dishes. The gentleman next to me shook his head, as if to suggest that I was talking about irrelevant matters. I may indeed have been talking of something entirely inappropriate, even ominous.

"So," I said, wiping away the tear-like sweat, "I would like to present the bride and groom with the Extraterrestrial as a gift. Please cherish it together."

I expected applause, but what followed instead was ambiguous silence. This was succeeded by an even more ambiguous commotion, which seemed like a tape that had sprung into action only to erase the meaning of my talk. A young woman next to me, probably a college student, asked me, "What shape is the Extraterrestrial? How many limbs does it have?

Upset, I said, "Four—the same as a human being."

"Oh, so it's like a monkey."

"No, it isn't. It has no hair—or tail."

"My, my," the gentleman next to me said. "If it is a human being, perhaps it's a patient who has run away from a mental institution."

That night I went to bed with the Extraterrestrial in my arms without L in the room. Mom and Dad had been too exhausted after the wedding to discuss what to do with it, but I knew the issue was bound to come up tomorrow. Dad seemed to be very strongly opposed to keeping it. Thinking of this, I felt as if all the blood would drain from my body from sheer anxiety. One possibility was to run away with the Extraterrestrial, as L had suggested one day. But that idea sounded so ridiculous I began to giggle. Nevertheless, I had to go somewhere. I kissed the lips of the Extraterrestrial, and breathing in the scent of nothingness, I was suddenly intoxicated. It was completely absurd that people called entering the dark universe "death." I would simply move to another world, probably through an entrance they could not see.

Toward midnight, I felt soft foot soles kneading my face. I realized L was sitting on the bed—with the most tender expression I had ever seen on her face—though she must have run away from something terrible of her own doing.

"Have you come back?" I said, offering her my hands. I felt the long-awaited consummation was at last at hand.

"No, we can't do it here," said L with a suggestive smile.

She flung apart the Extraterrestrial's legs, and, thrusting open the incredibly large vaginal opening even wider, tried to enter the Extraterrestrial's body between its legs. "I'll go first."

"It's like returning to the womb from which we were born," I said jokingly. L began to enter.

"My arms are stuck. Help me."

I cut a little around the hole with a fruit knife. Then L's body was swallowed into the Extraterrestrial at an incredible speed. Looking into the hole, I saw innumerable tiny stars and nebulae scattered in the dark space—and, among them, a tiny naked figure falling headlong like a comet and its tail.

We Are Lovers
(Koibito dōshi (1963))

Is it because I'm pure black that people resent me? It's true that my whole body is black—even if you turned me upside down and examined my groin, you would not find a single white spot. It was because I looked like an evil spirit that L, Yanni's "mommy," was so scared of me and detested me. She claimed that I was as ominous, filthy, and promiscuous as a black panther. She even said that what she hated most about me were my eyes, which looked up at her as insolently as any feral animal's.

L said this jokingly and said nothing more about me. The only reason she didn't go on complaining about me was that K, my "daddy," was her lover. They were engaged. Interestingly enough, K did not seem too fond of L's Yanni, either.

"You say Mika is pure black and eerie," my "daddy" would say, caressing my trunk, "but black is noble. Of course, I admit that to be pure white like your Yanni is not bad. He looks as clean as a virgin prince."

K, however, scarcely touched Yanni. Once K picked him up—immediately Yanni snarled, wildly scratched the back of K's hand, and bit his palm so hard it bled.

"Yanni, come on, what did you do?" said L, patting Yanni's head. And then Yanni lay down on his back, stretched his limbs against L's hands, and bit them. L tried to convince K that Yanni was just like any other adolescent boy, trying to attract attention by being tough. K began to laugh at L's efforts to soothe his pride. "He is after all a male. My Mika has never bitten me."

"Yanni always bites. Look at my hands, covered with scars!" L showed K her hands, to make up for the awkwardness the scene had created.

The truth was, however, that Yanni hated K, and the feeling was mutual—this is what Yanni told me afterward.

These circumstances were certainly not favorable for me and Yanni.

It was a five-minute run for me from K's apartment to L's, if I kept an eye out for cars and dogs. It would take Yanni only four minutes, he said. But when he came to our place for the first time, L was carrying him wrapped up in her white muffler.

"See? Isn't he adorable? This is Yanni, my baby."

"Since when?" As he said this, K held the blanket that covered me down tightly. With my nose and whiskers sticking out of the blanket, I gazed at Yanni.

"*Will you come here?*" I said. Taken by surprise, L dropped Yanni onto the floor. Yanni tried to crawl under the blanket with me.

"Is Yanni going to have a new friend?"

"Yes. In fact, I have a cat too," K said, giving up keeping the secret. "A female cat."

With this, K hauled me out by the neck, spreading my legs to show L that I was female. The unnatural posture and the embarrassment upset me, and I began to cry loudly.

"What a disgusting voice! Stop it, K."

K was always a tender "daddy" and was never rough with me. I gathered he did such a thing to hide his affection toward me from L.

"Is yours a boy?"

"Yes. Now Yanni, come here. K says he wants to hold you in his arms."

It was then that Yanni bit K on the hand with all his might.

While K and L were hugging each other's huge bodies, and licking each other's faces, Yanni and I retreated into the kitchen and ate some soup stock.

"*It's so tasty,*" said Yanni.

"*My daddy keeps it for me to eat between meals.*"

"*Do you mean K?*"

"*Yes. He's so sweet. He's not like himself today. Does your mommy hold you by the neck?*"

"*Yes, and she does even crueler things to me.*" Yanni bit the root of my tail lightly. It was so ticklish I began to laugh and crashed against his shoulder. Yanni, laughing too, crawled under my belly, trying to flip me upside down. As we played, Yanni told me about his "mommy," L. She would grab him by his legs and throw him into the air (and one out of three times she would not even try to catch him), and she'd drape him around her neck as if he were a white muffler.

"*I always sleep with L, and I wake up to find I am being held between her legs. She treats me like a fluffy puff of wool—that's how respectful she is to me!*"

"*You see, your mommy loves you,*" I said, knowingly. "*You like her a lot, don't you?*"

"*You silly girl,*" Yanni brushed my whiskers with his own.

"*You don't have to be embarrassed. I like my daddy a lot, too, and he likes me. He lets me sleep with him every night. Naked, he holds me with his smooth and springy arms to his hairless chest. He doesn't even get upset if I step on his face.*"

"*My mommy is gentle enough when she feels like it. She chews food and feeds it to me from her mouth. She always helps me bathe, too; Mommy likes to keep things clean.*"

"*Don't you catch colds taking baths like that?*"

"*She dries me thoroughly over the electric heater. It's so warm I feel as if I were in heaven. At night it's my turn to warm her feet. They're so cold—like twigs.*"

"*My daddy feels warmer than me.*"

"What's all this noise about?" It was L, coming into the kitchen. Seeing us entangled with each other and rolling on the floor, she screamed: "K, come here, quick! They're fighting!"

K lifted me in his arms and L picked up Yanni, glaring at me.

"*I'll come visit later. 'Bye.*"

"*Yes, you really must come back sometime. 'Bye for now.*"

As we said this, craning our necks, K and L pushed our heads down so that they could kiss each other above us quickly before parting.

I seemed to have fallen in love—with the pure white Yanni, of course. He was born in the same month I was. We were too young to plan our future, but I thought to myself I couldn't marry anyone else but Yanni. His long whiskers, sharp and masculine claws, green eyes, resilient and limber legs, the still tender and rosy peas on the soles of his feet, his graceful tail—none of these things could possibly fail to fascinate us female cats. And on top of all these charming qualities, there was that pure white fur!

I came to myself to find K gazing at me with a serious, reproachful look on his face.

"Have you lost your mind, Mika?" he said. "You can't let your heart get carried away by such a kid. It's just his appearance that makes him seem pure, clean, and noble. Men's voices crack at puberty. After that, they call their lewd calls and wander around outside, chasing women's rear ends. His fur will grow soiled and matted like a mouse's. No, it won't come to any good to you."

"*But, daddy, . . .*"

"Now, come to me. Let's go to bed."

K went to bed with me in his arms. The bed smelled of a big beast, which disgusted me. I tried resolutely to crawl back out. "Be good, Mika." Saying this, K wound my tail in his hand and pushed me back into the blanket, keeping me there with his arms around me. Giving in, I lay still on my belly, my chin resting on his arm. His thick hand moved slowly along my backbone—not the way it usually did, though. It moved mechanically, which suggested he was not thinking of me.

"*What happened to you, daddy?*"

"Do you love him?" asked K. "To love or not to love is not a question. If I was asked whether I loved her, I would have to answer no, I don't."

"*I love him. I do love him!*"

"Shut up, Mika, be quiet," K said in frustration, covering my face with his big hand. This had happened before, when L had visited him. K and L had been engaged since before I was born—since ancient times, so to speak. Nevertheless, they did not seem to be getting married yet. I thought that was the problem, though I didn't say so—it was none of my business. Besides, I did not want K to marry someone like L. I could never know what she might do to me once we started living together. I could not bear the thought that L, with that strange fragrance of hers, would sleep with K in the same bed every night, make me feel cramped, and worse, make me warm her cold feet. Still, if Yanni were there, too. . . . It suddenly occurred to me that if K and L got married, I could stay with Yanni. However, I was too concerned with K, who was looking exhausted and devastated, to think about the future for me and Yanni. Saying, "*Please, cheer yourself up!*" I licked K's nose and around his lips with my rough tongue.

It was on an evening some two weeks later that I risked walking secretly to L's house. I had memorized the route by following K when he visited L. Yanni had become remarkably masculine in those past two weeks, though his green eyes were as big and beautiful as ever. He drew his nose closer to mine.

"*Thank you for coming. It must have been dangerous.*"

"*My feet are hurting. Look how dirty the pads have gotten!*"

So saying, I sat and began to lick the bottoms of my feet. Yanni gazed intensely at the purplish downy hair below my belly. Unconsciously, I had assumed a seductive posture "*I like you a lot,*" said Yanni, trying to hold me in his arms. "*I am no longer a child.*"

"*No, stop it, Yanni!*" saying which, I tried to run away with my tail held vainly upright. I did not have enough self-confidence.

"*Please let me go for today. I am not yet as grown-up as you.*"

"*That's just an excuse. You don't have to be afraid of me.*"

We ran in a circle of black and white until Yanni succeeded in capturing my trunk in his lithe arms. I quivered with a pleasure that resembled terror, convinced that I wanted to have his baby, screaming it out, my claws raking the ground.

Suddenly, shrill laughter came on us from behind. It was L. Yanni and I were taken aback.

"You silly things! You're so clumsy at it!"

"*Mika, quick, run away! We're in trouble!*" cried Yanni in bewilderment.

"*No, I'm not going!*"

"Don't glare at me like that, Miss Mika," L said to me. "You look as though you'd like to devour me to the bones."

"*She's not like that, Mommy.*"

Yanni rubbed against L's legs with sorrowful eyes. L picked him up and caressed him under the chin and behind the ears with revolting tenderness. Yanni surrendered himself completely to L's hands, letting her push him up underneath her sweater. He seemed to have settled down between L's breasts and was taken home with a drugged look on his face.

"*I don't care anymore. I will never come and see you again!*" I cried, and ran straight to K.

The next day L came along. Ignoring her, I pretended to be asleep on top of the warm television. But she stretched out her long fingers to fold back my ears and pat my head. She said to K,

"Miss Mika came to see Yanni yesterday."

"I didn't know that. I thought she was home all day."

"They're in love," said L very coldly.

"How wonderful," said K, sounding as if it were a curse upon us. "It's no surprise. They have reached adolescence."

"I know. Yanni has been randy these days. Like you, he is an onanist." L burst out laughing. So did K, so hard his eyes were shortly filled with tears. "He wraps his legs around my pillow, imagining that it's Miss Mika, and repeats an odd movement. He looks strange, staring into the air. Then he wets the pillow a little. Have you seen Yanni's thing yet? It's so cute. When I turn him upside down and caress his belly, he almost closes his eyes, intoxicated. When my fingers reach the lower part, a rosy spear of asparagus appears among the dandelion fluffs like a miniature rocket."

"Has Yanni done it with Mika yet?"

"Not yet. Yanni is still a virgin."

"You should bring him here."

"Only if you don't mind."

"Why would I mind?"

"Because Miss Mika would get pregnant. Are you sure you wouldn't mind?" As she said this, L looked into K's eyes, her arms around his neck. The flame of a strange laugh beyond my comprehension would flicker in their eyes and draw their lips, which looked like the pointed heads of snakes, close together. Yet they would never suck each other. Instead, they would show their sharp tongues, and with these they would begin to tickle each other. They were very unusual lovers. As far as I know, they didn't do more than that even when they were in bed. Apparently both could not help laughing when caressed. It must tickle unbearably.

"I wonder why Yanni and Mika like to do such a thing," said L. "It's such a ridiculous thing to do."

"I know," K drew me close to him, pressing the peas on the soles of my feet to extend and retract my claws. "But we used to do that ridiculous thing very earnestly."

"Are we getting married?" L said, standing up. "There is no reason that we should get married."

"Neither is there any reason that we shouldn't." K said, and kissed me on the nose.

"I am going home."

I didn't know what to do—but perhaps I needn't have worried; it wasn't that serious to them.

After L had left, K crawled into bed. So did I, from the head side. He lay flat on his back, and I lay on his chest, feeling his big and warm heart beat with my belly. Then K lifted his head to gaze at me.

"*What are you thinking?*"

"I like you a lot, Mika." K said in a voice that sounded like an echo inside the bones. The grayish, empty-looking lenses of flesh were set toward me, though not actually focused on anything. Still, two images of me—my black face a little tilted—were reflected in his eyes.

He loved me, I thought. Of course, I had known that for a long time. Otherwise how would he have been willing to look after me from the days I could not even control my own excretion? I was heartily thankful for my daddy. But then, who was I to him? Why had he chosen me? Was it because I am sheer black, with glossy fur, one eye green, the other golden, with a well-shaped tail? It is true that K, unlike ordinary people, appreciated my nobility—the nobility of the black cat. But I didn't care anymore. What I cared about, what I felt proud of was my love for him, and his love for me. We had selected each other from our first encounter.

How I wished to confess all this to K! I wished also to shed tears. It was impossible, though.

"*I am your woman. I belong to you.*" Though I repeatedly said so, he just lay there, a gigantic existence one hundred times as big as I. "*I am not going to marry Yanni. I will stay with you forever.*"

I put my hands on his face, licked his lips, bit the bunches of hair in his armpits, and then ran my tongue along his chest and belly. It must have felt rough, rather than ticklish. As I went further, I ran into a big pillar of flesh. I was driven by the desire to eat it up. K would be mad at me if it were gone, though. So instead, I began to lick it tenderly. A quiver ran through his body. He held me tight.

When something warm splashed onto my face, I felt as if I were purified in ecstasy.

While I was out of bed, cleaning my face with my tongue and saliva, K prepared our dinner. I would be content if only he would feed me my dinner from his hand. After dinner, K watched the TV, and I lay on top of the TV watching K—waiting for him to say, "Let's go to bed, Mika."

The House of the Black Cat

(Kuroneko no ie (1989))

"I've rented a video from Kamiya. It looks interesting." When her husband told her this, Keiko replied, "Another homemade pornographic movie by Mr. Kamiya?" Kamiya, who had graduated from the same university as her husband, though a few years later, now worked for a TV station, as a producer. He also composed poems under a pseudonym. His award-winning anthology was—Keiko tried to recollect—entitled *The Black Cat,* if she's not mistaken. All the poems in it featured a black cat and dealt with a mysterious, apparently romantic relationship between a young man who appeared to be Kamiya himself and the black cat, "as noble as a prostitute, as coquettish as a dark goddess."

"I don't know if it's pornographic or not, but the video seems to be about the cat."

Keiko could hardly imagine Kamiya's work could be a straightforward portrayal of a cat's behaviors—it must be a visual version of the poems in *The Black Cat.* Keiko had made it a rule to watch such movies with her husband late at night, after her children had gone to sleep. For some reason, she felt awkward watching a provocative video all by herself, blushing and being aroused by it. It was a relief to have her husband beside her, for then it was just like watching movies or previews in the cinema with the rest of the audience.

The video *Black Cat* began with a shot of a house with white walls. The camera focused on a wall sunk in the pale, dim light of dusk or dawn. Then something like a charcoal line-drawing began to surface. Closer examination revealed that it was cat-shaped, and squirming slightly. It seemed as if a cat were in agony, confined in paint within the wall. This instantly reminded Keiko of Poe's "The Black Cat." She didn't much like that story, which featured the cruel killing of a cat.

"It's taken from Poe," said her husband, making the same connection.

One could never have become bored watching that picture of a cat moving and molding itself in the wall. Shortly thereafter, as the interior of the catlike outline was filled in with black, a pitch-black creature was revealed—and suddenly a pair of golden eyes was set aflame. No sooner had this occurred than a real black cat crawled out of the wall and came forward. The cat arched its supple back, drawing the Greek character omega—Ω—and then stretched itself.

Keiko gave a sigh of admiration. If it were a drawing, what an intoxicating curve that would seem!

"It looks more coquettish than the silhouette of a woman."

"Isn't it a woman in a cat's shape?"

"Its motions are exactly like those of a woman who just got out of bed."

This was true. There was something about the cat and its movements reminiscent of a woman languidly pacing around a room with the remnants of sleep in her disheveled hair. There were a skylight diagonally opposite the window, and a bed, a vanity table with three mirrors, and a chest, which the cat used as if they were its own furniture . . . and here, Keiko realized that miraculously, the cat was big enough to use the furniture the way a human being would—whether the furniture had shrunk or the cat had grown. Keiko took it for granted that the cat had become the same size as a human being. "This should be a woman in a cat figure after all," agreed her husband.

The black cat woman sat at the vanity table, with her glossy, hairy back to the screen. She raised her forepaws—or hands—forming a graceful diamond behind her neck, as if to comb her hair. Then she lined up cosmetics on the table and began to make up her face. How was she going to make up a feline face? Keiko took a strange interest. Did cats have lips to put lipstick on? As Keiko was wondering about this, the black cat took a light purple robe out of the chest, put it on, and walked out of the room on two legs.

In the next scene, the cat woman was sitting at table, having breakfast. It would no longer surprise Keiko to see her eat an omelet with a knife and fork and drink café au lait—in fact before Keiko had realized it, the cat-woman was doing just that. It would be even more natural for her husband or lover to be having breakfast opposite her—though Keiko was surprised, or rather, ill at ease, to find that he was human.

The man's back was to the camera, so the audience couldn't see how old he was or what he looked like. The cat-woman sat facing him. "What a beauty!" Keiko exclaimed again in admiration. It's a simple fact that some cats are prettier than others. A lover of cats since she was a child, Keiko had established standards for a cat's appearance. The face of this cat was so perfect it seemed as if it had accurately copied the ideal of cats in its profile and facial features. Especially its golden eyes, which had a slight green cast, were more beautiful than those of any woman. Keiko's husband sighed too. Keiko quivered unconsciously when the cat smiled at the man. The mysterious smile filled the viewer with the desire to be devoured by the cat.

Then the man disappeared—perhaps he had gone to work. What followed was a portrayal of the cat's everyday life. She now walked on four paws, jumped onto the windowsill, climbed the magnolia tree in the garden, and curled up to take a nap. The black cat had somehow shrunk to her normal size again.

When night fell, the cat grew as big as a human being again, and if Keiko had looked forward to watching the following scene, it was beyond even her expectations: an act of sexual intercourse of unearthly grace. It was not that the black cat was transformed into a human being, but with her cat's face and body, she embraced the man and made love to him exactly as any female human would. Keiko would never have imagined that a cat's limbs could so flexibly caress a person's body. Its rough tongue seemed very effective in this regard as well. The man's hand moved to stroke the cat's fur. Like any cat, she seemed to enjoy having her throat stroked. The cat's purring mingled with a song sung in a strange woman's voice, like background music. It sounded like a work by some contemporary composer, one that featured a soprano voice as a musical instrument, which would drive the listener crazy. The sound accompanied the physical movements of the exchange of pleasure. It seemed as if the cat woman were actually speaking erotically, while rippling the black curved line of her body.

The man's face always remained turned away from the camera. The pair began by making love in a standard position and then continued to move through one position after another. Eventually they assumed the beast's position. A part of the man's body seemed to be swallowed into the pitch darkness of the cat, rather than penetrating it. A long-lasting and high-pitched scream of pain or pleasure came as dawn's light broke abruptly through the screen.

"I wonder what technique he could possibly have used to shoot this?" Keiko's husband said in a voice dry with excitement. Her imagination too was so inflamed and swollen she was almost insensate. As was only natural in such a state, the couple couldn't do anything but reenact what they had just seen. Keiko tried to embody feline seductiveness, thinking of herself as a white cat when the strange music of a soprano voice began jumping in scat. Afterward, her husband said, "The white cat isn't bad, either."

For some strange reason, neither Keiko nor her husband was inclined to watch *Black Cat* again. They meant to return the video to Kamiya the next time he got in touch with them, but they never heard from him. Keiko's husband phoned the TV station and was told that Kamiya had taken a leave to travel abroad and had vanished without a trace.

"Is his wife at home?"

"He is married and has four children—female twins and male twins, I've heard."

"I'm rather worried. Why don't we go visit them someday?" Keiko said. She didn't like the idea of going by herself—something told her that something terrible might have happened.

It was on a Sunday afternoon, in the lingering chill before the cherry blossoms were in full bloom, that the two visited Kamiya's residence. The house they were looking for was built in the Spanish style, with elegant white walls. Dark red Japanese quinces were in flower, and a huge magnolia tree was swarming with blossoms in the garden.

"It's the same magnolia as in the video."

"It looks like that house with white walls at the beginning of it."

"Apparently no one's at home."

They were pushing open the wooden garden gate when they heard cats meowing above their heads. The black fruit-like things in the boughs of the magnolia turned out to be five black cats. As if to welcome the guests, the cats hung themselves headlong from the tree and climbed down to sit in a line on the white bench in the garden. The face of the biggest black cat looked familiar—this was undoubtedly the cat who had had sex with the man, the black cat-woman. Keiko was convinced that the cat's partner had been Kamiya—that this picturesque black cat must be his wife, and the other four his children.

"Where's your husband?" Without answering Keiko's question, the mother cat turned around and jumped to the windowsill, the others following her, and they disappeared into the house. From what Keiko and her husband could see of the inside, the house appeared inhabited. It didn't look like a deserted house whose master had taken flight. There was something unusual about the house though. Was it just Keiko's imagination that there was a slightly fishy, bloody smell hovering in the air? Was this smell from something the cats had eaten?

Her husband climbed in through the window and confirmed that no one was at home. The two decided it was time to leave. As they walked out of the garden and were taking another look back, Keiko thought she heard a woman speaking in the house.

"*I was so scared. They came out of the blue.*"

"Did you hear something, Keiko?"

"No, not really," said Keiko.

The Woman with the Flying Head

(Kubi no tobu onna (1985))

My father had a high-school classmate who was a little out of his mind. I never met him in person, only heard stories. Let me call him Mr. K for now. It was several days before my father died of a stroke that he told me about Mr. K's secret. (I wonder if the timing was pure coincidence.) This is not to say that Mr. K himself had hidden something from people; all his acquaintances knew about this "secret." It is just that my father had kept it secret from me till then.

This is a rough outline of the story.

I heard that since he had come home from China after the Japanese retreat, K had been repeatedly admitted to a mental institution and discharged. One day I ran into him in the street, and somehow or other it was decided that he should come to visit me at home someday. There is a legend that a scholar of the old school called Hyakken posted two verses at the entrance of his house. One was Ōta Nanpo's "Receiving guests is what troubles me most/ But not if the guest is you." The other was a spoof of the first: "Receiving guests is what delights me most/ But not if the guest is you."* Well I don't quite have the nerve to post the latter poem, but honestly, a visit from someone like K was about the least delightful thing I could think of. I did try to convey to him how unwelcome he would be, but K, a rather abnormal man, soon came for his visit. I remember this was before you were born.

Let me make it clear that K did not at all appear to be mad; there was nothing unsettling about his gaze, for example. It is true that he was gaunt and dressed like a vagrant, but that was not unusual in postwar Japan. But one could not help noticing the big, expensive-looking leather club bag he always carried in town. He had it with him when he came over to my house.

We talked about nothing in particular for a while, then he abruptly changed the subject.

"Do you know about the people with fantastic shapes described in the Chinese *Classic of Mountains and Seas*** and *The Account of Seeking Spirits?*"†

"The only ones I know about are the tribe of three-headed folk, the hairy people who were forced to work on the Great Wall, the giant who could swallow three thousand ogres—"

---

*The original poems read

"Yono naka ni/ hito no kuru koso/ urusakere/ towa iu monono/ omae de wa nashi."

"Yono naka ni/ hito no kuru koso/ ureshikere/ towa iu monono/ omae de wa nashi."

Both quoted in Uchida Hyakken, "Nichibotsu heimon" (1971)—trans.

***Shan hai jing,* a book of imaginative geography attributed to the legendary Emperor Yu of the Xia dynasty, annotated in the Jin dynasty (265–420).—trans.

†*Soushen ji*, the first extant anthology of ghost stories in China, edited in the Jin dynasty.–trans.

"You know them well. I am impressed! Among those strange tribes were the Aborigines with flying heads."

"Never heard of them."

"Their heads would leave their bodies and fly around in the middle of night."

"What a peculiar affliction."

"It was not an affliction that particular individuals suffered from. Everyone in the tribe, old or young, male or female, was like that. By the way, are you still single?"

"I got married last year. My wife has been out since yesterday, visiting her parents on some family business."

"I lived with a woman too."

"Why in the past tense?"

"This 'woman' was actually a seventeen-year-old girl. You know the one, the Chinese-looking girl, the one I brought home—or who followed me."

"I remember. Once you washed off the dust, she turned out to be an unearthly beauty."

"Well, eventually she grew up."

"That's only natural. I see, you became a Prince Genji, who slept with Murasaki, whom he had adopted and raised."

I made this joke having forgotten that K was out of his mind. But K did not seem offended; he just kept smiling, his indescribably sorrowful eyes like the winter sun.

"We couldn't get married. Li was my legally adopted daughter. Still, I sneaked into her bedroom one night. For some reason, she had wanted to sleep alone ever since she had been little, so we had always slept separately. Imagining what a sweet expression would be on her face while she slept, I couldn't resist the desire to visit her. Telling myself that I would be just looking at her face, I peeped into the chamber—to find she had no face."

"No face?"

"She had no head. I went completely pale, assuming that she had been murdered. Then I realized there was no blood. Moreover, even without a head her body seemed alive; her well-shaped breasts moved up and down, though I didn't know how she could breathe without a head. Between her breasts she was shiny with sweat. But still, she had no head."

"So she was one of the Aborigines with flying heads."

"You don't seem too surprised."

"Of course I am."

I was careful to try not to excite this mentally unstable man, for his story seemed to be coming to its climax.

"I was astonished. I was confused. All the same, I knew feelings beyond all morality had been aroused. My head felt overheated. Li was alive without her head, without consciousness or intellect. I touched her hand, which was warm and soft. It grew sweaty while I was grasping it. Beneath the quilt her legs were slightly parted. Li's legs were different from any Japanese woman's, long and straight, with feet as exquisite as ivory carvings.

"Nothing happened that night. Li was as good-humored as ever in the morning. There was nothing to suggest the extraordinary incident of the previous night. The next night it was the same thing—no development. Apparently, Li herself did not know that her head would leave her body and fly away. If she had known, she could have tied it down so that it couldn't fly away."

"Couldn't she tell if she had been molested while her head was away?"

"Her head couldn't tell, of course. Her body must have known, though. One night I finally lay with the headless Li. After that I had sex with her every night. Her headless body was like a sleeping body; it reacted vaguely when I touched it. In time, it seemed to learn a sense of pleasure; the movements of our bodies became well coordinated. One night Li's body shuddered in a different way, and her limbs coiled around me, clasping me terribly tightly. I nearly screamed in terror; I wondered if her head had come back and Li's pleasure was completed, or if some monster of carnal desire was trying to squeeze me to death. But I came back to my senses to find she still had no head. As always, the surface of her neck felt like a wet lip. I discovered that the headless body would surge with pleasure if I licked the wet part. Li's head never seemed to know anything about this. Her body was unable to inform her head of its nightly experiences."

"Where did her head fly every night?" I cut in. I could not bear to let him go on like this.

"Speaking of her head . . ." K snickered weirdly.

It is not pleasant to hear a lunatic snicker that way. "Her head didn't by chance visit a secret lover through the passage of dreams every night?" I said, trying to get him to finish the thought.

"You won't believe this. One day, with a serious expression, Li confessed to me, 'Father, I have fallen in love with someone. I dream of secretly visiting him every night.' Of course it wasn't me she was in love with."

"And you were overwhelmed with jealousy?"

"It's not that simple. I felt like any father of a grown-up daughter, or like Prince Genji when Tamakazura, one of his adopted daughters, was taken away by General Higeguro. But honestly, I felt like saying to her, 'Is that so? Well, you've grown up and now you love someone. Go, get out of here and marry him. But leave your body here. Only your head is allowed to go.' "

"That's terrible."

"I didn't actually say that to her. All the same, Li began to cry. 'I can't marry him,' she said. 'He's already married.' "

I felt I couldn't stand to listen any longer. Once more I urged him to finish the story.

"You are right," he concluded. "I was as jealous as anyone in such a position. One night, in a fit of jealousy, I did a terribly stupid thing. Toward dawn, Li's head came home from meeting its lover. For the first time I saw it fly: it flew like a big bee, using its ears as wings—I hear that's how the heads of the Aborigines with flying heads flew. Her head looked excited and joyful, and this enraged me. In an instant, I covered her body with the sheet so her head couldn't reattach itself. Her head looked distressed and fluttered about, but it did not ask me for forgiveness. It seemed in agony. 'Look at yourself—you deserve it!' I thought. Before long, Li's head stopped breathing."

"How could you be so cruel!"

"I know, but by the time I felt regret for what I had done, it was already too late. Almost instantaneously, Li's head grew dry, wrinkled, and shrank to an incredibly small size. Here it is."

So saying, K opened that bag that was so ill-suited to his shabby clothes and took out the head—I didn't have time to stop him. I almost screamed. It looked like an earthenware head. Once one looked at it, it was hard to look away. It was especially hard for me—before my eyes was what remained of the unforgettable face that made its flight to see me every night it was alive.

That, of course, is what my father did not tell Mr. K. The head of the beautiful Li flew to my father every night. The first time, he heard something like a bird brushing the windowpane, and a sound like a kitten mewing sweetly. Though my father spared me details I can imagine how they conversed, when he'd let it in and stroked the chilled hair strewn along the desktop. I could not look my father in the face while he was telling me this. "Your mother never knew about this. I thought I should tell you someday, because, . . ." My father hesitated.

"Let me finish with K first. After K 'killed' Li's head, her body remained alive for several days. Before it withered and died, a baby girl was born from the headless body. K was arrested for raping and beheading his adopted daughter, but he wasn't prosecuted because he was diagnosed to be schizophrenic. I adopted the girl and raised her as my own daughter. That's all I have to tell you. I haven't dared examine you to see if you've inherited the disease."

After my father's sudden death, I repeated this story to myself time and again. For now I have no lover, nor have I met one in a dream. I don't think my head has yet begun to fly. It shall not fly—until the day I fall in love.

The Trade
(Kōkan (1985))

It was on a business trip to another prefecture that I met the man. I had gone to a meeting with prefecture officials and some from the local headquarters of the ministry I work for. There were no important issues on the agenda; it was just a dull exercise for formality's sake, at which we were to reach prearranged agreements. I thus had leisure to examine the faces of the participants carefully (there were quite a few from the municipal government) as they sat around the rectangular table.

The face that first caught my attention, whether I liked it or not, was that of the man in question—I shall from now on refer to him as "Mr. Akujō"—who was seated in the lowest-ranking seat.

His face was so malignantly ugly that you could never forget it once you had seen it. It occurred to me that he would have good reason to hide his features behind a Noh mask, the mask of the goblin called *akujō* or *beshimi,* or better yet, a frowning *akujō,* for his face was even more beastly and deformed—so much so that it was difficult to look on with a steady gaze. While it is true there is no shortage of unsightly-looking men, I had never seen such a positively inhuman face. Nonetheless, I couldn't resist the impulse to peek at him repeatedly. He must have sensed this, for he looked back at me self-consciously and seemed to acknowledge my gaze with a faint smile that played about the corners of his mouth.

As I recollect that first encounter now, however, I believe that for his part Mr. Akujō could no more help watching me than I could him. At the risk of sounding vain, I must state that my looks are the exact opposite of his—my beauty has never failed to attract the attention of both men and women. Utter ugliness and utter beauty were linked in an intense gaze, each somehow aware of the perfect contrast.

Perhaps this made me feel close to him. I filled a glass for him at the welcoming party held by the municipal government, and he poured one for me. We even exchanged a few words. I forget what we talked about—nothing particularly personal, I believe. I found Mr. Akujō enjoyed being among people, which came as something of a surprise to me. In fact, as long as you avoided looking directly into his face, he was a perfectly unobjectionable companion. He was bright enough, and there was nothing diabolical or abnormal about his disposition, despite his grotesque features.

Some two years later, I received a telephone call in my office. I could not quite place the caller's name.

"I met you the year before last, when you came to our prefecture as a visiting official," he said. Still I could not remember who he was. Then he added, slightly ironic, "I'm the one with the unforgettable infernal face, you know."

These words recalled that face, if nothing else, immediately to my mind.

Mr. Akujō explained that he had come to Tokyo and had business he wanted to discuss with me. As it was official business, he should have come directly to my office; however, he worried that my colleagues might be taken aback by his looks. He did not wish to inconvenience me, so he suggested that we meet at a club or some such place that evening, if I did not mind.

I was about to decline, uncomfortable at the thought of taking him to a club I frequented. However, he designated a club himself and jokingly said, "I may not be much to look at, but I am rather popular with the girls who work there; they find my face distinguished and alluring." Though I didn't much like his informal tone, I made an appointment to meet him that evening.

Mr. Akujō appeared overjoyed to see me; he was in an extremely good mood and drank at a steady clip. The extraordinary face left me mystified as to his age. Judging from what he said about himself that evening, he appeared to be far older than I and, to my surprise, was even married.

"How can a man with such a face be married—that's what you are thinking, right?" This question made me uneasy. A young hostess stroked his face, saying, "It's not that bad. It's like a mask, a cute little monkey mask."

"Go ahead, touch it. See, it's as tough as wood."

She's right, I thought. The flesh of Mr. Akujō's face looked as firm and glossy as a blood-black mask.

"You, on the other hand. You're so handsome I almost hate you," the tipsy hostess said as she tried to caress my face. I couldn't suppress a look of peevish impatience. This stiff demeanor of mine, along with my too beautiful face, was part of the reason that in spite of my looks, I was really not all that popular with women.

"As a matter of fact," Mr. Akujō said, settling into his life story, "I have a family just like most men, because I used to look different. If I say so myself, I was as handsome as this gentleman."

The girl gave a shudder. "Weird!"

"Yes, I was so beautiful that it might have seemed almost

weird. Then, one fine day, my face was suddenly like this."

"How scary!" shrieked the girl.

"Don't you want to hear my story?"

"Sounds creepy, but interesting."

This was Mr. Akujō's story: One night he had a dream, in which appeared a man with an incredibly ugly face. Saying that he had a favor to ask of Mr. Akujō, the man told his own story:

He had made a business trip to a mountain village near the border of his prefecture.

After finishing up his business, he rowed up a mountain stream, hoping to get in some fishing before going home. He came to a place where flowering pomegranates were clustered all around, so that the banks blazed blood red, as if in flames. Making bold to step out of his boat he came upon a small cave. Deep in this cave hung a sheer diaphanous screen, with light gleaming dimly beyond it. The man boldly thrust aside the gauzy curtain and continued on, until he came out into a dazzling light-filled world. Magnificent villas in traditional style lay scattered among well-cultivated fields. It seemed to be no particular season here. Peaches, plums, and all kinds of unfamiliar fruit grew together in the orchard. He heard dogs barking and roosters crow somewhere.

"Just like the 'Account of Peach Blossom Spring'* of Tao Yuanming," I said. Mr. Akujō nodded in agreement. "That's what I thought in my dream. According to the man, it was a world apart from this one, in which time does not pass. There were no children, everyone there seemed to have lived there thousands of years. And all of them had

---

*"Taohua yuan ji," a tale written by Tao Qian [Yuanming] of the Jin dynasty—trans.

such well-formed features that it seemed marvelous."

"And I suppose that after several days' hospitality there he went home to find that many years had passed?"

"No, not like that. The man told me that the people there had suggested that he stay there for good, and he was coming to like the idea himself. But by the riverside one day he saw what looked like hundreds of reversed masks hung up as if to dry. As he lifted one and turned it around, he realized that it was an actual human face. Every one of them was hideously ugly. They felt lukewarm as if alive. A scream burst from his throat, and throwing the face down, he fled this 'Peach Blossom Spring' without once looking back. But when he was safe, lying among the pomegranates, he discovered that his own face had somehow been transformed into one of the terrifying faces on the shore."

"That's the story of the man in your dream?"

"Yes, but that's not all. When he was done telling his story, he asked if he could exchange his face for mine." As he told me this it was as though Mr. Akujō himself were the man in the dream, asking me to exchange my face for his. He grinned at me strangely, and it seemed to me that he was looking longingly at my face.

"So what did you do?" the hostess asked.

"Naturally I refused the request. And the man left without a fuss that day. But he appeared in my dreams every night after that, demanding to trade faces with me. The man said he could live in 'Peach Blossom Spring' if he succeeded in getting my beautiful face. 'How can you be so selfish,' I said to him. 'What on earth would I do if I were deprived of my face?' The man smiled at my shudder of disgust and said that I should know better—I could find a handsome man to make the same exchange that he had. And he declared that he intended to trade his face for mine whether I gave my consent or not. The next morning when I woke up, my face felt swollen. When I got up, my wife fainted at the sight of me. The long and short of it is that I'd had my face traded away without being able to say no and ended up with the one you see now."

The hostess gave a shrill cry. "You're kidding!" she gasped, distraught. I too thought that Mr. Akujō must be kidding, to scare the girl—or to be more precise, that's what I decided to think.

A few days later I had a dream. When I awoke from it, I thought it might have been terrifying enough to transform my face or turn my hair white. Mr. Akujō had appeared in it.

"I probably don't need to tell you this," he said, "but I've liked your face since the first time I met you. I have considered many others, but none of them is as desirable as yours. I won't rush you, but I will be back to ask for your consent another day. I hope you will agree to my request—I know it may cause some inconvenience to you at first, but as I suggested the other day, you in turn can find someone to trade faces with. Thank you for your consideration."

With these words and a chilling leer, Mr. Akujō left. He may return as soon as tonight. I will accede to his request and am looking for a partner to trade with.

The Witch Mask

(Kijo no men (1985))

My family has a strange heirloom. It is neither a historical artifact such as a scroll of calligraphy, an antique, or a sword, nor a jewel with some market value. It's not a memento by which our ancestors established the family's social or financial status. I am the only person that looks on this piece as a family treasure. Neither my grandfather nor my father told me about it; I just happened to discover it hidden away, completely forgotten, and kept it as my own treasure.

It is the horrific mask of a witch. At first it seemed to be a Noh mask, and I took it to be the mask of a *hannya,* or a witch, though I didn't have any deep knowledge of such masks. Years later, however, I realized that it was not the face of a jealous woman such as Namanari or Hashihime in "The Iron Ring,"* but that of a terrible witch—nothing more or less than that. It looked like the witch in "The Autumn Foliage Hunt,"** for example—but even more like some witch older than the bloody witch of the Edo period.

---

*"Kanawa," a Noh play. An entire translation of the work by Eileen Kato is included as "The Iron Crown" in *Twenty Plays of Nō Theatre* Donald Keene, ed. (New York: Columbia University Press, 1970), 193–205.—trans.

**"Momijigari," a Noh play attributed to Kanze Nobumitsu (1435–1516).—trans.

It was also a size bigger than a Noh mask—that is, it was just big enough to completely cover an adult's face. And there were no eye holes. In short, this mask was not for Noh plays.

It was a grim dark color, as if it had been soaked in blood and dried, over and over again. When I looked at the witch mask in my dim study in the rain and chill of early summer, the wooden skin grew wet, as if it were perspiring. The mask had come alive again and turned into a witch's face. The skin was moist with the sweat or—as appeared more likely—blood that oozed out of the flesh. What was even more uncanny was that the dark wooden surface seemed to me to take on a hectic flush. It seemed the witch mask had come back to life, to express a will of its own. I also noticed that just like a Noh mask, its expression would change from every angle; raging at one moment, deriding at another.

I have, by the way, never to this day put on the mask myself. I have tried in vain to wear it. The reason is as follows: while it is true that masks generally appear grotesque and ridiculous when we look at them from the reverse, I had to hold my breath from sheer revulsion when I first turned the mask over. The darkness—a darkness made of flesh, so to speak—was gleaming from the reverse side. It looked as if the mask had snatched shreds from the face of someone who had worn it, and made that flesh part of itself—and as if that bloodstained, ragged surface had crystallized into a darkness as black as lacquerware. Gleaming with phosphorescence in the darkness were the two eyes of the witch. As I told you, there were no eye holes. Light then from the real world could not have brightened those eyes through the mask: they must have been glimmering with light from the other world.

As I contemplated the mask in my hands, I was tempted, perhaps by that mysterious gleam, to put the mask on. But when I drew my face close to the mask, the darkness on the inner side growled, baring teeth and trying to bite my face. Driven by terror, I pushed the mask aside with all my strength and looked away. I had come within a hair's breadth of being bitten by the mask, and I was still aware of a remote echo in my ears, as if it were that terrifying witch on the other side of the darkness growling.

Considered objectively, there was nothing unusual about the terror I experienced. Except perhaps for those cheap, thin masks for children, any mask might produce the impression that it would never let the face go if one were careless enough to put it on. If my memory is correct, the French writer Maurice Mergle once composed a poem, "The Mask of a Samurai," about a mask that attached itself to a woman's face. In any case, I had learned my lesson and from that time on was discouraged from putting on the witch mask. What occurred to me was a different idea altogether, and as the years went by, this idea took root in my mind and grew into an irresistible desire.

When I was in college I had a girlfriend, like everyone else. I'm putting it modestly; in fact I was quite popular with the female students. Several of them were seriously interested in me. None of them were the frivolous type; they were well bred, conservative, and studious. I was also a bright and bookish student—at least on the surface, apart from my secret desire. I believe I can say that I was conscientious in my dealings with women.

When I was about to graduate, I decided to select one of these female friends as my future wife—or to be more precise, it was decided for me. We were engaged by the exchange of betrothal gifts and planned to marry in a year and half, when my fiancée was to finish her bachelor's degree.

This woman—let me call her K-ko for now—stood out among the female students I dated around that time because of her graceful demeanor. She was intelligent and reserved. Yet she was capable of becoming unexpectedly passionate—I am alluding to her behavior in the bedroom—a hidden trait in keeping with her voluptuous body, which one would not have guessed at, seeing her fully clothed. We quite naturally became involved with each other after our engagement. Our relationship grew progressively more intimate, our techniques more exquisite and ambitious. In short, we were something between a married couple and lovers, passionately desiring each other's bodies.

My parents had passed away by then, and my younger brother having inherited our property in the countryside, I took over a house in Tokyo that my father used to use in business. I earned a position in a government ministry. As a recent university graduate I was thus quite well off. Though a housekeeper who used to look after my father stayed in the house, she was almost completely deaf. Not counting her, I virtually lived by myself. K-ko frequently came to stay with me over weekends. Her father, by the way, was a university professor, who would take a "liberal" position about moral issues.

It was a rainy Saturday evening in autumn. K-ko had fallen asleep beside me—it had been as mesmerizing as ever, or even more so. I was well content with this soft white slumbering creature and was sure I was in love with her. Still, I was haunted by an idea—the call of the demon (I cannot hold it back from you any longer), the desire to put the witch mask on a beautiful face. And there an ideal beauty slept, eyes peacefully shut, her face turned toward me—that face looked like the mask of the *waka onna,* the young lady in the Noh repertoire. What might happen if this "young lady" were covered with the "witch"? I knew the mask would probably cling to her face, but I could not imagine what effect it would have on the woman herself. My mind was reeling from its struggle with the "call of the demon."

I took out the witch mask. Hardly aware what I was doing, I laid it on K-ko's face—and it clung there as if by the witch's will, or some magnetic force. K-ko sat up as if she were still asleep, unaware what had happened. She made as if to uncover her face, tugging at the mask with her hands, but it seemed the mask would never let her face go. K-ko staggered to her feet. The jerking of her arms as she struggled to take off the mask was accompanied by a sinuous swaying of her entire body. Gradually this movement of her naked body turned into a sort of erotic dance. A cat would dance madly in fear if its head were covered with a bag. This beauty, her face transformed into that of a witch, performed an unrehearsed dance, her unveiled body swinging to a strange rhythm. I do not even know if one could call it a dance—perhaps she was writhing in agony. But the sound of her voice—if she made any sound—was absorbed within the mask and could not penetrate it.

The sculpted body under the witch's face soon grew flushed, as her dancing became more intense. The strangely graceful movement of the flesh was at the same time incomparably obscene. Completely out of my senses, I could not wrench my eyes away for an instant. I might describe it this way: the witch mask seemed hardly to move, to be fixed in space, as if it had, so to speak, pinned or perhaps crucified the woman's face there, creating a center around which her sleek body danced. The conviction grew in me that the dance expressed some surpassing pleasure, or sexual ecstasy; the horned demon's face was, strange to tell, inflamed with bloody rapture. The demon's gaping maw looked as if it were silently screaming with delight. Then with a great orgasmic convulsion, the witch fell to the floor, shook her bare breasts and belly, threw out her limbs abruptly, shuddered, and suddenly stopped moving. K-ko was no longer breathing. Appalled, I rushed to prop her into a sitting posture, and when I did, the witch mask fell from her face as if it had never been stuck there. K-ko had been delivered from the mask by death. Her face did not betray the least trace of agony; she wore the antique smile of a Buddhist sculpture.

K-ko's death was attributed after an autopsy to "cardiac insufficiency," or heart failure—a misfortune for which I was not held at all responsible. I mourned for her as would any unhappy man who survived his fiancée. And it is true that I grieved her death. However, one thing was clear: what preoccupied my mind was not sorrow but the unforgettable memory of that dance unto death.

It took me a year to formulate a strategy, and then I began dating a woman whom I will call M-ko. Three more months passed before I carried out my plan for the witch's dance. This was necessary for me to convince myself that M-ko was a fit companion for me. Her dance was less graceful, probably due to her slim physique, but the beastlike violence of her movements and the raw obscenity of her gestures made it even more spectacular.

After M-ko, I decided to forgo the process of building a relationship or becoming engaged to the woman. I took an invaluable suggestion from the movie *The Collector,* which I happened to see at about that time. Since then, I have become a "collector" who catches and chloroforms "prey"—my "sacrifices" to the witch mask now occur approximately twice a year. The main difficulty I face is how to do away with the body. I will spare you such details for now, however, for I have described them in a book to be published in due time. The only thing I might add here is that though I am not a connoisseur of boys, on a whim, I once chose a beautiful lad for sacrifice. The result was almost as I expected. There protruded something like the long bill of a water bird throughout the dance, ejaculating intermittently until the dancer drew his last breath.

All that remains in my mind, a clearly drawn picture occupying a corner of my brain, is the thought of putting the witch mask on my own face. I feel as if the golden eyes of the witch smile at me seductively every time they see me.

Spring Night Dreams

(Haru no yo no yume (1989))

Cherry blossoms in full bloom torment Ms. Saiko. It's not that she is allergic to them, as many people claim to be these days. It's that she feels the blossoms will entice her, that the halo of their color will grow in her head and intoxicate her, until her body goes floating alongside her. In short, she almost becomes a sleepwalker.

"So I am afraid of walking under cherry trees in full bloom. Especially the *somei yoshino* cherry, which blooms before growing any leaves. Under the hazy moon it looks as if it is going to shed some mysterious spirit."

"In other words you are lured by blossoms into a dream world," Mr. Sakai teased her. "'Longing for the moon/ covered with the fragrance/ of the cherry blossoms/ I cannot even see/ my dreams clearly now'*—isn't this how you feel?"

"Isn't that Teika's poem? It does convey a mysterious atmosphere, but my mood is a more serious affliction."

"Oh Saiko, psycho, psychic, psychedelic, psychosis," Sakai said, as if reciting a verb conjugation.

Saiko glared at him, but smiling.

---

*The original poem composed by Fujiwara no Teika reads "Hana no ka no/ kasumeru tsuki ni/ akugarete/ yume mo sadakani/ mienu koro kana" (*Shoku go shūi waka shū,* 1326, 2 [Spring 2]: 130).—trans.

Her problem went beyond what she described to Sakai. What Saiko couldn't comfortably confess to Sakai was that an affliction of her psyche was developing inside her. Each spring for the past few years this affliction had tended to grow stronger than ever. As the days got warmer and more and more blossoms came out, a lump of illusory emotion grew in her heart. Saiko admitted that this emotion, which grew and developed like a fever, was in fact jealousy. The season of blossoms was a season of jealousy for Saiko.

It was five years ago in autumn that Sakai had begun to pay nighttime visits to Saiko. Their relationship had continued since that time, Saiko always waiting at home for Sakai to come, and come he did, irregularly and yet incessantly, several times a month. When he appeared it would be suddenly, in the middle of the night. Saiko understood that it was very difficult for them to get together in any other way, owing to Sakai's job and status. All she wished was for him to come more often—preferably every night. In that case, one might think, it would be most reasonable if they lived together. This was, however, impossible as well. Sakai already had someone, whom Saiko, with respect and complex emotion, referred to as "Madame." Further, if by some chance Saiko were ever to be married to Sakai, she couldn't imagine herself looking after him as Madame Sakai did, and living with him in the same house. She didn't think she could live with anyone—not even Sakai. She couldn't escape the need to live alone in her own cozy nest. Nevertheless, she desired that Sakai come every night.

He couldn't, however, not only because he was extremely busy with professional activities, wife, and children, but also because he had several lovers. Sakai didn't deny their existence. And Saiko didn't ask about them—at first. After all, Sakai first made his appearance to Saiko like a huge comet that had capriciously shifted its course to chase her. In his normal orbit, several stars already had their places. This seemed to Saiko too natural to all concern at the fact that this comet went around visiting one star after another.

"It's all right that you keep several mistresses besides myself," Saiko said to Sakai one day.

"It's quite unsettling to hear you say that."

"You employ them, then, if it sounds too vulgar to say you 'keep' them."

"I cannot get rid of them easily, because of a number of complicated circumstances, so to speak. I should have known better and signed contracts with them for specified terms. But I must ask you to be thoughtful and understand."

"Yes, sir, I am thoughtful and do understand. It has nothing to do with me," said Saiko, laughing. Sakai echoed her laughter.

"If it causes you trouble for me to visit you this way, I can 'keep' you anytime—anywhere you like, in this country or elsewhere."

"I am a little tempted to be kept by you, but it is surely best to go on this way. Come and see me patiently, inconvenient though it may be for you."

"I feel as if I were a man in the days of the old imperial court."

"Yes, and I assume I am receiving a secret guest like Prince Genji."

"It's fortunate that you are a princess living in a corner of this big estate; I can visit you secretly at night."

"How about following your model, who lived a polygamous life in his Rokujō Palace, and moving your wife and mistresses into this residence to live together?" Saiko almost said in jest, but she managed to restrain herself.

Saiko's residence was located in what was formerly a

suburb of Tokyo. The premises were so spacious that its corner encompassed a trace of the Musashino coppice, and several old cherry trees still bloomed in spring. Within the estate were her parents' house, a house for their eldest son, Saiko's brother, and his family, and Saiko's own house. She lived with a Thai "lady-in-waiting" in a half-timbered pseudo-Tudor house that her grandfather had built in his last days. Saiko called it "my hut." She'd had a study with a skylight added to the hut after she'd returned from abroad and been appointed assistant professor at a university; she wanted to watch the moon and stars above her head as she wrote novels at night. Saiko had been regarded as "a talented young writer" ever since winning a prize for new writers when she was in graduate school. She would teach and meet people in the daytime and at night would usually stay in her "hut" to write. Thus it had scarcely ever happened that she was out when Sakai visited her unannounced. But the real reason she'd stopped going out at night was that she wished to wait at home for Sakai's visits, which could never be predicted in advance. Saiko was aware of her own motivation and didn't think highly of herself for being so preoccupied with Sakai.

"I never know when my prince will come."

When Saiko mumbled this, listening to Keith Jarrett's "Someday My Prince Will Come," Sakai promptly drew lines through the word *Prince* in the printed lyrics, and substituted *King*.

"I am too old for a prince. And besides, I might become more prominent," he said.

Gazing at him as if taken aback, Saiko said, "The best you could expect is to be promoted to prime minister, isn't it?"

"If kingship is too much to ask for, then is this within my reach?" With this, Sakai crossed out *King* and wrote down *Erlkönig*.

"Ghost king. . . ." Saiko sighed. "That's about what you are—appearing and disappearing like a spirit, always in the middle of night. I'm so frightened of the ghost king's visit every night that I can't write properly. And once he comes, he holds me tight and drains all my energy, so that I can't do anything but fall into a dead sleep. What shall I do about you?"

Sakai listened to Saiko, looking at her tenderly, and then he began to say something strange.

"Once upon a time, there were the Three Beauties of the Land, as they were known. You could be one of the three today; the Three Beauties of olden days included Empress Somedono."

"I know about her. She was a daughter of Councilor Fujiwara Yoshifusa, and she was compared to cherry blossoms. What does she have to do with me?"

"She has something in common with you: both of you are unearthly beauties. It happened that a distinguished Buddhist monk, Shinsai, a disciple of Kūkai, fell in love with the empress at first sight. This somehow became widely known. Shinsai was troubled, and ashamed, and died shortly thereafter. Monks were supposed to attain nirvana, but that wasn't how it happened with him. Alas, he was transformed into a demon of a deep blue color, and he haunted the empress."

"Then what happened to the blue demon and the empress?"

"I don't know. After all, he had been a monk—he must have become a Buddha eventually, thanks to prayers."

"So what do you mean by telling this story?"

"It's just that I was on the point of becoming a demon, blue or red, just like the monk, when I saw you and fell for you head over heels."

"If you had become a demon, I would have kept you beside me and fed you—what a shame."

Saiko laughed as she said this. Looking at her smiling face, Sakai said, "It looks like I am going to be served a feast tonight, too."

Saiko made it a rule to "serve him a feast" when Sakai came. This demon, blue or red, was always hungry and ready to devour her. This was merely the explanation Saiko liked to offer, but she suspected that she herself was a witch with a voracious appetite, who could never get her fill of devouring Sakai's body at every opportunity. Whatever the case may have been, the two would hold a feast, eating each other's bodies, usually until dawn, when Sakai would leave.

How did she get there? Saiko wondered, lying in the bed where Sakai had left her countless times. She was taken by surprise, hypnotized, dazed by some powerful love potion, and raped. That was, to her mind, closest to the truth.

It was at the party held to celebrate her winning the new writers' prize that she had first met him. Looking back now, it was still unclear why Sakai had even been present at the party. Several days later, he wrote to her that he would like to come and see her. Saiko did not respond. Sakai did not say a word about it, though they happened to see each other at several social functions. Because he kept smiling at her, Saiko returned the smile. Several months later, Sakai suddenly came over to her house one evening. He somehow convinced the Thai maid that he was entitled to enter Saiko's study. Before she realized what had happened, she had already been conquered by him. She couldn't have done anything anyway; she found the invader smiling in front of her. When he talked, she was hypnotized. When she kept silent, she was dosed with an aphrodisiac of words. Eventually she was bowled over by his confessions of love. The rest went on as if she had voluntarily agreed to do what he wanted to do. She gave up herself to this person, be he "prince," demon, or ghost king. But looking back on what had followed, it was not he but Saiko who had been transformed into something like a demon, waiting to catch the other on his next visit.

Saiko felt her first attack of jealousy, which would rise to fever pitch during the cherry-blossom season, when an article reporting the existence of one of Sakai's mistresses appeared with the woman's photograph, in a weekly tabloid. Told of the article by someone who did not know Saiko was involved with Sakai, Saiko took the trouble to buy a copy of the magazine. She fell ill at the first glimpse of the article. It provided her with information many times more detailed than what she had previously known about Sakai's wife and family.

"I read an interesting article about you."

When Saiko told him this Sakai laughed, as if to hide his embarrassment. "I have lost face. It was such an ordeal." Despite his words, he did not appear chastened. Saiko was appalled by his lack of sensitivity.

"I promise that I won't upset you like this again."

"I won't mind—I have become numb."

But there was something else she did mind. "Madame" aside, Saiko could not but mind the existence of mistresses other than herself. This was evidenced by the outbreak of symptoms of jealousy and sleepwalking in the season of cherry blossoms.

Another item of gossip had exploded like fireworks this spring. It was reported that another of Sakai's mistresses had borne him a child. Again Sakai managed to get away with admitting that his sheer lack of virtue was responsible for this. That, it seemed, was a truth that everyone simply had to accept, Saiko included. There was no point in blaming him for his lack of virtue or discretion. Whatever he might say, Sakai was nothing but Saiko's lover.

When she felt an acute pain in her chest—a sign that the lump of jealousy was growing rampantly—Saiko would look at her face in the mirror. It did not look like her face at all. It appeared that someone else's face had intruded from the other world, the world beyond the mirror, and had stuck to her own—it was as if her face were covered by a mask. The more she looked at the "mask," the more it became the mask of a witch. When she widened her eyes and distorted her mouth, her face in fact resembled nothing so much as that of a witch. "I have finally become a demon." Mumbling this to herself, Saiko felt as if she were about to be swallowed by the mirror, and she tottered unsteadily before it.

From that time on, Saiko was able to change her face into the witch's as she wished, whenever she was alone. When the transformation occurred, she would feel something like a cold mask fixing itself to the flesh of her face. Simultaneously, a strange sensation would surge through her, as if she had been given a witch's magical powers. She felt as if her body, existing outside herself, could float anywhere while she dreamt.

One evening, Saiko dozed off while in her demon state—which was dangerous. She heard someone recite, as if chanting a curse, "I am never at ease/ in a spring sleep;/ the cherry blossom, short-lived,/ is blown by the winds/ even in my dreams."* Outside, a fake-looking moon shone. The night was as bright as if it were false daytime. Lukewarm breezes scattered the cherry blossoms liberally. Mirage distorted this forged space. Saiko realized that her body was

---

*The original poem composed by Princess Shikishi (or Shokushi) reads "Yume no uchi mo/ utsurou hana ni/ kaze fukeba/ shizugokoro naki/ haru no utatane" (*Shoku kokin waka shū,* 1265, 2 [Spring 2]: 147).—trans.

floating through space and had arrived almost in the same moment at the home of the mistress who had given birth to Sakai's baby. What was she going to do to her? As a witch, she should be able to possess women and children with no difficulty, shouldn't she?

Strangely enough, Saiko remembered clearly every detail of the scene—from the mistress's room to the face of the newborn baby, which looked like that of a monkey's fetus. Seeing Saiko, the woman gasped like a beast and expired. The baby had a spasm and grew still too.

On wakening, Saiko found that in the world of reality it was still night. The petals of the cherry blossoms streaked by at fantastic speed in the moonlight outside the window.

Saiko went into the bathroom and soaked her entire body in hot water. As she did this, she happened to notice fallen cherry blossoms floating in the tub. It seemed as if she had wandered naked, and while bathing, she shed blossoms. Her face was still half that of a witch. By massaging it vigorously and continuously, she brought back her ordinary features.

Sakai did not show up for a week or so.

"I have been given a hard time again," he said without explanation when he at last appeared. His smile, as attractive as ever, was an incomparable gift to Saiko.

"What happened to you?"

"Don't you watch TV or read magazines at all?" Sakai observed her face. "That mistress of mine who had a baby died suddenly. She died from some mysterious shock, and the baby died at the same time. The police interrogated me, but I was not in Japan for the three days around the incident, fortunately or unfortunately."

As they lay talking in bed that night, Saiko told Sakai about her strange experience of a week or so before. She told him that it must have been she who killed the woman and her baby. She even confessed to Sakai that her face in the mirror would sometimes resemble the face of a witch. But Sakai did not seem surprised to hear her say these things.

"I am afraid I may appear to your Madame at any moment and show her the witch's face. Anyone who saw that face would be frightened to death. Not even you would be an exception."

After a pause, Sakai said to her, "I have thought for some time that any ordinary woman would die if she saw that face of yours. But I won't—I have been used to it for some time now. I knew all along that your identity was a witch's."

"Have you seen the face?"

"I am looking at it right now," Sakai said jokingly. "Take a look in the mirror."

Saiko's face in the mirror flittered as if made up in a mirage. Then from under her flesh, the mask of the witch surfaced. Saiko cried out.

"As you are an honest person, you have shown this face to me. Yet I have kept coming here without fear. It's not bad to have a demon lover."

All that Saiko could do was to whisper through her tears as he held her in his arms, "If you were to stop coming to see me, I would become a real demon."

The Passage of Dreams
(Yume no kayoiji (1988))

It was two months after her remarriage that Itsuko first dreamed of her late first husband. He looked quite fit as he always had, which was impossible for a dead person. Itsuko was overjoyed at the encounter, and yet it filled her with sadness as well. It was as if the bottom of her heart had been removed and sorrow oozed into every cell of her body. She realized that however healthy he might appear in that dream, she could never live with him again.

The scene that surrounded them seemed like one that could be found somewhere in Tokyo. Itsuko worried that she might look even more ghostly than her husband; her hair, blown by the breeze, was long on one side and short on the other, just as it had been when she was a schoolgirl. She was carrying her violin case, as usual. Mr. Minami, her dead husband, was walking a little ahead of her, the familiar-looking flute case in his hand. Perhaps they were going to dinner after a chamber music concert, thought Itsuko in her dream. In her dream, when she quickened her pace and caught up with him, she didn't know what to say. Knowing that he was after all a ghost, she gave a sidelong glance at his face, which appeared to be made of the dark flesh of the dead.

The city also looked unearthly. Skyscrapers and airships seemed to sway, as if underwater. The other people in the crowd—yes, the streets were very crowded—were like strands of seaweed undulating in the water, looking two-dimensional and insubstantial. She grew anxious and wanted to call out to her husband, when the water stirred wildly, the city collapsed, and she found herself awake.

In her dream the next night, Mr. Minami was on the television, performing with a jazz piano trio in a club. In the dream, Itsuko entered the TV with no difficulty and found herself already seated up front in the audience. Mr. Minami was playing a jazz version of "Toccata" from *Pour le Piano* by Debussy. The live music bubbled in Itsuko's body—something that had not happened for a long time.

The two came together again that night, sleeping in the same bed and making love as they had done innumerable times. Though a sober cell remained in the corner of her brain and kept asking her in a whisper how she could do this with a dead man, Itsuko lost herself in the arms of her late husband. Her whole body was turned into a flute of flesh and played improvisationally; winds of music swirled through it. Itsuko could not get up the next morning for some time, as if she had really slept with her late husband and was worn out from their night together.

Every night after that, Itsuko had a secret rendezvous with her former husband. It was fortunate that no major recital had been scheduled in the near future, because she realized her spirit was melting away with remarkable speed. Mr. Kamiya, her current husband, would not overlook this; he was a doctor. Itsuko decided to confess her nightly experiences to him.

Mr. Kamiya, forty-five years old, had been a widower for ten years. He said that he had loved Itsuko's performance in London three years earlier and since then had attended her recitals whenever possible. It was only recently that she had been introduced to him. A recording company executive had said to her in secret, "Someone wants to be your patron. Why don't you meet him, just once? He said he would like to take you out and treat you to duck."

In fact, Itsuko loved all kinds of fowl. She ate whatever flew in the sky—thrushes, pheasants, ducks—cherishing the creatures at the same time. She loved fish nearly as much; they were almost like birds, gliding through the water with their fins rather than flying with wings. But she couldn't stand the meat of land animals; the smell of it overwhelmed her.

No sooner had the two sat down at the table and exchanged greetings than Mr. Kamiya made a marriage proposal. "Well?" Itsuko said, her eyes wide open like a young girl's. She was not taken aback or annoyed by this unseemly abruptness. This gentleman is asking me if I will marry him, she thought, reflecting on it as if the whole thing concerned someone else. She didn't think about what her answer would be. The two began to dine and chat as if nothing had happened. Conversation flowed back and forth over the table in a graceful whirl.

"Don't you recognize me?" Mr. Kamiya asked, "I always sit up front at your recitals." Itsuko looked straight into the handsome face of a middle-aged man one might find at a salon frequented by Virginia Woolf.

"I'm sorry," said Itsuko, tilting her head, "I hardly ever look at the audience—the seats look dark and uncanny, crowded with beasts holding their breath. I try not to see them; when I perform, I close my eyes and enclose myself in a pearl-colored sheath that I create around me. That's not good. I should make your bodies vibrate with the resonance of my violin. Maybe I'm not really talented enough to be a performer."

The gentleman shook his head in disagreement. "By the

way, I haven't told you anything about myself," he said. "At least let me give you my business card." The card informed Itsuko that Mr. Kamiya was a neurologist.

"What a scary profession!"

"Smells of blood?"

"No, not that. It has a botanical fragrance—the scent of bamboo, for example. That reminds me of something. Long ago, Wang Huizhi or someone else referred to bamboo as 'this gentleman.' Pale green, slender, and cool as crystal, its sophisticated appearance makes bamboo an appropriate metaphor for a virtuous gentleman."

"You honor me far beyond my merits by this comparison. To what then shall I compare thee? To the orchid, perhaps, if I were to choose from the plants named 'the Four Gentlemen.' "

"A more childish flower would be better for me. Something like . . ." But Itsuko couldn't come up with an appropriate suggestion.

By the time the dinner was over, she had accepted his proposal. She was amazed by how calm she seemed. It's as easy as agreeing to a recording contract, she thought to herself. As for Mr. Kamiya, Itsuko simply smiled at him and said, "All that I ask is to be spared the wedding ceremony and reception. I will notify city hall and send cards to my friends saying 'I am married. I will continue to use Kojima Itsuko as my stage name.' "

"That's fine with me. Move in with me whenever you like. I'll see to it that the house is ready for you by the end of this week."

Ten days later they were legally married. Itsuko felt a little mesmerized, what with this bamboolike gentleman asking for her hand. Her friends in the music world would often tease her, calling her "the Dreaming Fairy." The nickname was even more appropriate now—she looked as if she were walking in a sea of clouds. Despite her disposition and excitement, she managed everything meticulously. She delivered herself to Mr. Kamiya as if she were a piece of merchandise purchased by an enthusiastic customer and ended up sleeping in the room next to his. They decided to keep the custom common to both of them from their previous marriages—to sleep separately.

What delighted her last and most in her everyday life was to enter her own bedroom after wishing her husband a good night's sleep. It was especially delicious to throw her heated body into bed after "the midnight sun"—that was how Itsuko referred to sex. She had liked to visit her former husband's bedroom. Sensing her preference, Mr. Kamiya decided to lure her into his room.

"How did he do it with his late wife?" Even though the question often preoccupied her, the Dreaming Fairy was neither skilled nor enthusiastic enough to interrogate her husband successfully. She simply had him show her a photograph of his previous wife. She looked completely different from Itsuko, a brilliant-looking beauty with a sharp visage. Itsuko felt that perhaps she may have played the piano. This was the only question she asked of her husband, but he answered "no" with a shake of his head.

Mr. Kamiya seemed unaffected by his previous marriage; he might have just wed for the first time. This was not so for Itsuko, though. It was only three years earlier that Mr. Minami had been killed in a car accident—and moreover, he had lately been coming to her every night in her dreams.

"How are things going with Mr. Kamiya?" asked her former husband one night.

"Things are just fine," replied Itsuko calmly. At the same time, she wondered how he, now residing in the land of the dead, could know about her present life. She had thought that in her dreams she had been seeing him in the past.

"I mean, how are you 'performing' with him?"

"Oh, that." Itsuko blushed and lowered her long eyelashes. She gave a diffident answer to the effect that it takes a long time to produce a satisfactory musical performance when one has changed partners. Deep in thought, his arms crossed, Mr. Minami, however, did not look convinced.

In fact, Itsuko had never reached orgasm when she had what Mr. Kamiya shyly called "bedroom things." Quite the contrary, she couldn't rid herself of the sensation that her body had been penetrated by something strange. The "gentle" husband would transform himself from the virtuous bamboo into a fat snake whenever they touched each other naked. Her body came nowhere near vibrating and sounding like a flute. Itsuko felt sad, even though her husband was infinitely sweet and treated her as carefully as if she were a broken doll.

"Just as I thought. Things don't seem to be going well," said Mr. Minami, as if he knew the sexual secrets of the newlyweds.

It's your fault, Itsuko was about to say—but stopped herself from talking any more about her new husband.

The next night, Itsuko finally consulted Mr. Kamiya about the troublesome dreams.

"I don't know whether I should call them nightmares or not, but I feel sorry for you, Doctor." Itsuko had gotten used to calling her husband "Doctor" when she was being formal. She liked the dependent tone in which she uttered the word.

"So how does Mr. Minami look?" Mr. Kamiya asked with equal formality.

"He looks fine, just as ever—he seems to have his body and to live a life in the other world. I don't know who would tell him what is going on in this world. He comes to this world and enters my dreams."

"He must have found the passage to this world," Mr. Kamiya declared.

"Yes, it's not that I visit the other world, . . ." So saying, Itsuko became uncertain. Did not the city, room, sky, and sun belong to the realm of the dead? Neither the urban scenery nor the people floating in it looked earthly.

"In classical Japanese poetry it is called 'the passage of clouds.' In one poem the speaker commands the winds to close the passage of clouds to keep the heavenly virgins in this world. In your case, however, you should block the 'passage of dreams' to keep the dead from this world."

"How could I manage to do that?"

"I can't help you. I may be a neurologist, but I can't cut open your brain and build such a barrier."

"Please just try."

"I was just kidding. All I can do for you is to prescribe a sleeping pill."

However, Itsuko did not allow him to; sleeping pills might affect her body and eventually her performance.

Mr. Kamiya took a leave of absence to accompany Itsuko on a performance tour of Europe in the summer of that year. Having successfully completed the last recital, they checked into a hotel in London. When Itsuko came back to her own room that night and went to bed, Mr. Minami showed up again in her dream. She woke up immediately—the dream disappeared like the image on a TV screen when the set has been turned off. She'd thought that her visitor must have vanished too, but it wasn't so; she felt a presence from a different sphere lingering there—the ghost of her husband. Though she had never been afraid of Mr. Minami in her dreams, Itsuko was frightened now that he had oozed out of the dream as a ghost. Not wanting to go and get her husband, who was fast asleep in the next room, Itsuko watched the ghost from her bed until the morning, her body frozen in place.

She told her husband about the ghost at breakfast. "I didn't think he would follow me abroad."

Mr. Kamiya laughed. "Of course he would. A ghost wouldn't need to get on the airplane, and he wouldn't have to pay."

"How could he get all the way to London, then? Do ghosts fly in the sky, like birds?" Itsuko moved her arms childishly, imitating a bird beating its wings.

"I'm afraid ghosts don't have wings."

"Then do they fly like squids, with their hands together above their heads?"

"Perhaps they cross the sky like vapor trails," replied Mr. Kamiya, and changed the subject, telling Itsuko how he had first seen her in London three years before. He asked her if she remembered what she had performed then.

"I cannot forget that you played, in your typical trance, Schnittke's *A Paganini,* Rochberg's *Caprice Variations,* and Ravel's posthumous sonata and *Tzigane,*" he told her.

"I know it was an odd program."

"You looked so cute, like a living doll with slender arms playing the violin. As I listened, desire was aroused in me: I wanted this doll. It took me three years to get it."

"Am I still a doll, over thirty years old?"

"Dolls never age," Mr. Kamiya declared.

The next night, their last in London, Itsuko again saw her deceased husband in a dream. This, however, was a dream of a different sort. Itsuko arrived at the appointed place to find Mr. Minami chatting with a woman around thirty years old. The smile on his face made Itsuko sense that they had been emotionally involved. The woman had long hair and a sharp visage; she looked like an actress or a fashion model. Itsuko thought she seemed familiar, but in her confused mind she couldn't quite identify her. Somehow Itsuko became the wife of Mr. Minami again—she was so devastated by his infidelity that she felt as if all the organs had been removed from her body.

Mr. Minami finally noticed Itsuko. He waved off the woman, who disappeared in a moment. They were in a club crowded with dead customers. The smoke and the smell of the dead almost suffocated Itsuko. Coming back to her senses, she realized that she shouldn't have come to such a place.

Mr. Minami seemed to be wearing an extra layer of skin on his face. This was the face of a man determined to break off a relationship, thought Itsuko. He lit a cigarette and said, as she had expected, "You shouldn't come here anymore. I want to end things between us now."

"You've found someone you love in this world. Is it the woman who just left?"

"She is the pianist who has agreed to perform with me."

"Then why don't you introduce me to her?"

"I can't do that."

"But I want to ask her to take good care of you."

"Then I should appear to Mr. Kamiya and ask the same thing of him."

"That wouldn't work."

Suddenly, Mr. Minami lifted Itsuko in his arms and carried her to bed. This was going to be their last duet, Itsuko told herself. Her body was transformed into a flute and began to resonate as usual. This time, however, the winds of breath did not swirl through her body; instead, the flute of flesh became inflamed and filled with a tearlike fluid.

The flood of tears melted her flesh, even her eyeballs. No music was heard any longer.

Itsuko emerged from her dream, worried that she would wake up with swollen eyes. Looking at her face, Mr. Kamiya said, "You look like an actress who has just played an overwhelmingly tragic scene."

"I cut the tie with him finally."

"Now the passage of dreams is blocked."

"Thanks to you," she said with a feeble smile, trying to sound unconcerned, but she began to wonder why her husband seemed to know everything about her dream.

She was daydreaming as ever in the airplane back to Japan, her big eyes wide open, when all of a sudden, she exclaimed "Uh!" in a clearly audible whisper.

"What happened?" Mr. Kamiya turned to her.

"I've remembered who the woman last night was." Itsuko told him the gist of the dream from the night before, excluding the "performance." "The woman was your former wife, Doctor. I'm absolutely sure."

"What an interesting story. You have as much talent for story-telling as for music."

"Are you saying that I make up stories and dream them?"

"Don't look so fierce," said Mr. Kamiya, laughing. "To be honest with you, I just may have been a cowriter of the scenario of your dream. I guessed she was the woman in your dreams last night. It seemed likely that she would get to know Mr. Minami in London—she was killed in a car crash just by Heathrow International Airport ten years ago, when she was with two members of a TV commercial production company. I understand it was a terrible accident. If she lingered around there, she might well get to know Mr. Minami when he came to London."

"This sounds pretty fantastic."

"Anyway, if she holds on to Mr. Minami, he won't come into your dreams. You will be able to sleep well from now on. Isn't it all for the best then?"

Itsuko felt mesmerized, as if in the spell of a magic show. The more she thought about it, the stranger the story became, coherent as it might at first seem. Had "the doctor" asked his former wife to help him out? Did he keep in touch with her? If so, by what means? Question after question came to her in a torrent, though she stopped herself from asking them.

Itsuko wished to look into Mr. Kamiya's mind, into the brain of this man who himself specialized in the study of the human brain. She sometimes thought that men's brains were fashioned in such a complicated way that they hid mistresses, spies, refugees, criminals, and more beyond the reach of women's imagination. Men's brains seemed able to control more than one mistress simultaneously. Women could never understand how men's brains could carry out such complex activities.

After saying this to her husband, Itsuko asked, "What do they call the thing that remains mysterious to outsiders?"

"The black box."

"Women's brains are structured so simply that every corner is visible to you. Right, Doctor?"

"Whatever you say. Their bodies, on the other hand, are like labyrinthine musical instruments; I have no idea how to play them well."

"May I offer a suggestion? In the case of my own body, you should blow rather than fiddle or press. If you could blow to make it vibrate, it would sound fine. It seems I am not a stringed instrument or keyboard after all, but a flute."

Itsuko told him that she didn't really like the sound of the violin. It didn't echo inside the body; rather, it sounded externally and made one's ears prick up.

"I want to have the sound inside my body—the best thing I can think of would be to become a mouth organ or a pipe organ myself."

Perhaps Mr. Kamiya took this hint. When autumn approached—just as the poem reads: "The fan by which I brought a breeze/ now itself is blown by autumn's wind,"* Itsuko began to sound well in Mr. Kamiya's arms. She was again aroused by the sensation that her body had been transformed into a flute. Overjoyed, she became as wild as a hooked fish, as energetic as a bird soaring into the sky.

"I worry that your former wife will grow jealous and come to intrude on us," she told her husband.

"Don't be afraid; she is not that type. She would never trouble others," said Mr. Kamiya. The way he said it made Itsuko wonder if a secret line of communication still remained open between him and his former wife, whether it was possible for them to discuss and conspire about anything. Perhaps his dead wife could be compelled to do anything Mr. Kamiya asked—like attracting Mr. Minami in the dream in London.

Itsuko then felt strangely close to her. She wanted to see her again and pleaded with Mr. Kamiya to show her the photograph of his dead wife once more.

"I wasn't mistaken."

"So it was she?"

"Yes," and as she said this, Itsuko also answered her own question about whether this woman had blocked the "passage of dreams" at Mr. Kamiya's request.

---

*The original poem by Fujiwara no Yoshitsune reads "Te ni narasu/ natsu no ōgi to/ omoe domo/ tada akikaze no/ sumika nari keri" (*Fūboku waka shō,* c. 1310, 9 (Summer 3): 3403).—trans.

The Special Place
(Erabareta basho (1988))

Kei had come down to the seashore in early summer with his cousin Mai. "The sea in August, at the end of summer, makes one feel lonely, but the sea in May, before there are many bathers, has a similar effect. It is like a fruit that is still tough and unripe. It seems to me that as summer ripens, something significant may begin to happen."

"It does seem that way," said Kei. "People swarm about devouring the ripe summer, then leave summer's corpse behind."

"And then by the time the dry winds begin to blow both the sun and sands have whitened, and the sea begins to look like a graveyard."

The two were lying under a beach umbrella, both naked. Kei lay on his back, Mai on her belly. Kei took a sidelong glance at Mai's back, curved like the keel of a vessel, and her firm hips, to which grains of sand had stuck, a microcosm of the galaxy.

Perhaps it was not his business to suggest outright she should wear her swimsuit. On the other hand, he felt just as awkward not suggesting it. Kei quit trying to make a judgment and closed his eyes. Though Mai had packed a bathing suit to bring to the beach, she had decided not to go swimming in a sea that she had found still too cold. Saying that it would be tiresome to change into a suit to sunbathe, she stripped completely naked in front of Kei's eyes. There was nothing provocative about her manner, though. She took off her clothes with the naturalness that comes from a certain kind of indifference. Strangers rarely appeared along the sandy beach between the two capes that looked like a pair of dinosaurs, a stegosaur and an ankylosaur—the beach was private property. Nonetheless, it would cause a bit of trouble if they were seen by Grandfather or any of the other relatives.

Shō, Kei's first cousin and three months his elder, had complained of a sore throat this morning and stayed with Grandfather and Keiko, his mistress. This was the reason that it was Kei who had accompanied Shō's elder sister Mai to the sea with the beach umbrella and other equipment in his arms. Kei wondered to himself if Mai could have been as indifferent with her own brother. But the soft breeze and the sound of waves dissolved Kei's wandering thoughts. He felt he was wrapped in a gauze of sweet slumber.

When he came to his senses, Kei found what he thought were sea lice assembled about his head; they had apparently come from a fissure in a nearby rock. On closer examination, they appeared to be a group of ambassadors from a foreign country. They stood in dignified ranks, and the one who looked like their representative made a speech to Kei. The sound of waves in the background made it hard to hear him. But it sounded as if they had come to meet Kei at their king's behest.

"Are you taking me to the Dragon Palace?" As he asked this question Kei sat up. "I hope you'll excuse me. I don't like being underwater."

"We are not fish, and neither is our king the Dragon King," said the messenger, a little indignantly. "We are philosophers who dwell in the metaphysical world."

They looked too dull to be metaphysical, though—as dull as capricorns could be, Kei thought to himself. But without knowing how he found himself walking along the road into the sands, guided by the group of messengers. He felt as if his body had become considerably smaller. The sands lost their substance, looking like they were a cloud or a mirage. Kei crossed something like a desert or a gaseous heavenly body. Shortly there came into sight what might have been a contemporary city with skyscrapers, or an old-fashioned castle town. But it looked like a stage backdrop, a mere drawing done in feeble lines. A great swarm of people, like bees or ants, was moving in the streets, but they also looked as insubstantial as line drawings.

Kei was received by high-ranking officials, as befitted a guest of state, and ushered into the palace, where he was guided to the king's throne. The king was slim and looked like an ageless Taoist wizard. He must have been extremely old, given that he was a philosopher king, Kei thought. Then the king began speaking. An interpreter conveyed his message to Kei: This was a special land, and Kei had been invited as a special person. Not quite understanding the message, Kei expressed gratitude for the high regard that the king had shown him and asked, via the interpreter, if he would be allowed to ask questions. The king nodded.

"You are granted only three questions though," the interpreter said, passing on the king's decree.

"What is the name of this country? Where is it located? For what purpose have I been invited?"

The answers to the three questions were: The country is called Kaloon; It is located in the subconscious; You have been invited to marry the princess and rebuild the country in its decline.

In reply, Kei set three conditions, saying he would not

assume the task unless they were met. First, he wanted the marriage canceled. Second, he wanted to be exclusively responsible for the rebuilding of the nation. And third, he wanted the king to let him go back to the world he belonged to.

Unexpectedly, the king accepted Kei's conditions without any objection. It was conveyed to Kei that to rebuild the nation meant to build a new city based upon a free plan. This castle town, it was further explained, was aging and had lost its vitality. The city was losing its flesh and being transformed into bones; it would become increasingly abstract until it was a mere tangle of lines. It was in its final phase. If one pulled on the outline at a certain point, the city would lose its form and be reduced to a single straight line, like a thread coming untangled.

"Your mission is to disentangle the threadball of the declining city and then to use it to build a new city. You are not allowed to cut the thread; you must preserve its continuity."

An idea occurred to Kei immediately. The current city plan consisted of rectangular spaces of different sizes, but the city in Kei's mind was a simple, circular structure made up not of concentric circles but of a spiral sequence of circles, like a conch shell. Imagining the beautiful circular city that would emerge in the special land, Kei was overjoyed.

Then he was guided to the princess, who lived in another wing of the palace. She looked as old as Kei, or a little older. She was a beautiful girl, drawn with a line of chill, as befitted the daughter of a philosopher king. Her face reminded Kei of Mai's; both girls resembled a noble dog—like a stoic scholar. Except for a soft cloth that wrapped her body like a robe, she was naked.

"I hear you declined the marriage proposal, Kei," she said, without any change of expression. Apparently she could speak Kei's language.

"It's not that I declined it. I am going to leave after my work is done. I will decide what to do about you then."

"I like that. But you can't get away from here, Kei. All the princes brought here have been confined within the cities they built, and there they died. But you are different. All the others tried to marry me as my father decreed, but you gave a conditional answer."

"Now that I have seen you, I feel I should have given him an unconditional answer."

"You don't have to be considerate," the princess replied, smiling for the first time. "It's I who have come to like you. I will try to help you in some way."

"Thank you. And what are the conditions?"

"There are none."

"That's interesting. Then I can suggest some. When I succeed in building the circular city, I will take flight with you, and we will get married in my world."

"That's only your wish. It cannot be a condition to offer me; I don't want such things to happen."

"You're saying that you won't run away with me?"

"Because it's impossible," the princess said calmly. "First of all, I probably wouldn't be able to live in a world as dense as yours. So you don't have to be concerned with me. My life is not restrained here, though it will continue to be boring."

Kei thought perhaps an hour here might equal a year in the world he had come from. Or would several decades here be no more time than it took to steam millet in his world?

While Kei was preoccupied with such thoughts, the princess carelessly dropped the cloth that covered her upon the floor and stood there naked.

"Why don't you strip and make yourself at home?" Following her suggestion, Kei stripped naked as well. This must be the custom in this country, he thought. Asking the princess if this was so, Kei was told that members of the royal family would remain naked even in the presence of servants and dressed only for rituals and meetings with foreign ambassadors. When attending such events they would cover their bodies with the minimum breadth of a cloth. The naked body of the princess appeared to Kei such an intelligent body, like a theorem of geometry demonstrated by drawing an additional line of the minimum necessity. When she walked around the room the movement of her body seemed to be a mental exercise. Kei didn't know how to rule the princess.

After a while, the princess stepped on the simple bed, inviting Kei to take part in the ritual of sharing the bed. Kei became cautious; he had set the king the condition of not marrying his daughter. He should not respond to her allure too easily, or he might end up bound to become the king's son-in-law. The princess, however, exposed her body to him imprudently and urged him to come to bed.

"Come play with me, and don't worry. Never mind what you promised my father," said the princess, "for he will not keep his word either."

On hearing this, Kei stepped upon the bed and began to solve the theorem of her geometry, drawing lines in his own ways. The princess resisted, trying not to be solved. Eventually, however, Kei overpowered her, analyzing and conquering her completely.

Talking in bed afterward, Kei told her of the circular city he would draw. He intended to confine the king in the middle of the labyrinth, which would be of spiral form, caving in gradually toward the center. Then he would kidnap the princess and flee to the world he had come from. While talking about this, Kei was fidgeting with something like a thread that he had found underneath the pillow.

It was too thick to be a strand of the princess's hair. It was too fine to be rope. It had unusual elasticity; Kei was able to pull it infinitely, out of nowhere.

"Stop playing with that, or everything will collapse," the princess warned in a dreamy voice. But soon she was breathing deeply, fast asleep. Driven by curiosity, Kei kept drawing on the thread or line, whatever it was. When he was worn down by an almost overpowering boredom and felt his eyelids about to fall, the room suddenly collapsed. First the whole palace and then the entire city fell in on Kei's body. They were unexpectedly light, so that he wasn't crushed to death. However, he could not move his body under the accumulation of lines, which looked like a tangle of a thread. Beside himself, Kei cried out. . . .

When he woke up, Kei found his body covered in sand. His entire body, except for his face, seemed to be lightly veiled with sand. Still in the posture of being crucified, Kei called out to Mai.

"Are you awake now?" As she said this, Mai looked into Kei's face. "Where have you been, and what have you been doing?"

"I dreamt I visited a city called Kaloon. And you were the princess there, Mai."

"You are a liar. As punishment, I have buried you except for your face, and that other part of your body."

Having said this, Mai walked away toward the villa, leaving Kei behind. She walked exactly the way the princess had walked in the dream.

Flower Abstraction

(Furawā abusutorakushon (1991))

When Cousin Shō came by, Kei was drawing a picture.

"It's a feminine sort of picture. What is it?"

"It is a flower abstraction," Kei replied.

"So it's a picture of a flower."

"And of a woman, too."

"So is it then an abstract painting of the image of a flower and a woman?"

"Does it appear that way to you, too, Shō? An American woman painter born in the last century—Georgia O'Keeffe—did many floral paintings in this manner. It is called 'large-scale flower painting.' Flowers come to look strangely abstract when they are painted as if they had been enlarged by a close-up lens. I'm imitating O'Keeffe here."

"You and your intellectual talk! I don't know whether it's about a flower or what. But you can't view it as anything other than a woman's parts—not a girl's, but an adult woman's—once the association occurs to you."

Kei continued trying to create different hues of rose. "It's true. In the one you're looking at, the areas of dark rose and blood may appear to be a cave into the center. But it's an abstraction of a rose. If you became an insect and crawled inside a rose, the flower-chamber would appear that way. Now what do you think the one I'm drawing now is? Does it look like the bud of maidenhood?"

"Let me see. . . . This one looks too complicated."

"Doesn't it? I mean it to be a landscape painting. Ravines, hills, and clouds growing above them—all made of petals and floral fragrance."

"I feel as if a trick were being played on me. Still, it looks to me like the entrance to a female body—or an exit to it, if you will."

Kei liked chatting with his cousin Shō, who was three months older. Active and not as studious as he might be, Shō collected an amazing amount of information from hearsay. He was good at tuning into Kei's intellectual talk and developing it into humorous dialogue. And he and Kei had one taste in common: both loved young women. They competed with each other, each striving to become more advanced than the other in the study of women.

Kei stopped painting and began putting away his brushes. "By the way, where are you taking me tonight?" he asked.

Feigning a lack of enthusiasm, Shō mentioned a hot pop singer. "I might be able to go dancing with her. I don't think you would like her, but I came here to pick you up, if you're interested."

"Thank you for your consideration. But to be honest with you, I'm not fond of a rodential type like her."

"Rodential! What a pedantic way to put it! But you're right; she is like a squirrel, cute but meager-looking. The only good thing about her is that she's energetic. Well, if you're not inclined to go see her, I won't either. It's started to rain too."

"I like rainy evenings—unless I'm out. I like to be at home, listening to the sound of rain outside, drinking tea and indulging in meditation. . . . Shall I ask my mother to make some weak tea?"

"You sound like you're seventy years old. I'd rather drink bourbon and lose myself in fantasies."

"I have some. But my brain would go numb before I reached that stage."

They were chatting this way when the "student-in-residence," as Kei called him, brought them drinks.

"What is this? It's sake, but it tastes as sweet as a Sauternes."

"It's a recreation of the sake that they say Rai San'yō liked to drink, according to a three-hundred-year-old document. It tastes amazingly sweet and is appropriate for young men to drink while discussing girls on a rainy evening, as Prince Genji and his friends did in *The Tale of Genji.*"

"But it seems pretty strong for young people."Shō contemplated the cut-glass wine cup curiously. "This cup must be made from an old design."

"Not really. It's just a faceted wine cup made in a traditional Edo style."

"Grandfather was talking about 'the cup filled with the night light,' I recall."

"About the white jade cup that would fill with sweet, fragrant liquid when left out in the yard at night, right?"

"I don't know if it was a jade cup or what, but it looked like soiled marble. I prefer this one."

"Don't drink as if you were drinking whisky. You need a chaser."

"No need to bother. I would rather like to be informed of your recent achievements, if I am not too hasty." Shō affected to speak like a politician. Shō's father, who was Kei's uncle, was a politician. When the two young men discussed something embarrassing, they would speak in the language of the adult world. If Shō spoke like a statesman, Kei talked like a businessman. Their common grandfather, Mr. Irie Akira, had been active both in politics and business.

"As for that," Kei said, holding the glass cup near his

mouth, "nothing remarkable has occurred in regard to the matters I've been telling you about. Which is most unfortunate, I might add."

Shō laughed. "Such a lapse is inexcusable," he said. "Hasn't the beautiful girl who did away with the madman in Saint-Tropez come back yet?"

"It seems her father took custody of her in Paris."

"That's a shame. But I am looking forward to seeing her. From the likeness of her face reproduced from the display, she was a genuine beauty. I am also attracted by her waywardness. But she is not the subject of the painting you have just shown me. It's an ordinary metaphor, but she is like a lily."

"I would compare her to a moonlit beauty."*

"Well, I'll leave floral metaphors to you, the flower specialist. How about the girl who watched you sometime ago over in the mansion in the snow?"

"She seemed like a fox in disguise. And she is under the control of Grandma Keiko. I can't do anything about her. You speculated, Shō, that she must have sprung from the Gion area. But I can't see the fox girl unless I visit Kyoto again."

"You like ghostlike girls, Kei."

"'Ghostlike' is an exaggeration. You should say, 'fairylike.'"

"Much the same. I would rather keep my distance from dangerous girls. I prefer girls who are healthy and animallike."

"One could have more sound relationships with them," Kei said approvingly, "except that you have too many of them."

---

*The Japanese name of the flower of *Epiphyllum oxpetalum*, a species of cactus, is *gekka bijin*, which means "moonlit beauty."—trans.

"I have secured as many girls as I could, considering meanwhile which ones I might pass on to you. But I have charge of far fewer girls than the quarry you have taken in with your computer network."

It sounded as if Shō were comparing Kei to a spider. That was a little inaccurate, Kei thought. Kei didn't draw his prey in to eat them. Connected to him by his electronic spiderweb were numerous brains. Kei the spider would suck the honey of information produced by these brains, and in return massage them with messages. These brains in response would tremble with pleasure, spasming from the excess of excitement. In comparison, verbal and physical communication on the field of action seemed as roundabout as scratching one's foot through one's shoe. In the case of physical contact, one could only indirectly massage the brain through the impediment of the body. But by Kei's method one could directly caress the naked brain.

"Is that so?" Shō asked, only half convinced. "I don't share your taste. You are a super computer, and thus can fall in love with computer brains. I am only interested in the appearance of the box that holds the computer. All that counts for me is the color and design of the box—and that's especially true when it comes to girls."

"It's not that I deny your point. Indeed, I am extraordinarily concerned with the design of boxes. But I would call them flowers rather than boxes. Women are flowers, you know."

"I see. That's why you are engaged in flower collecting."

"I am interested not only in collecting flowers but also in transforming myself into an insect and exploring their insides. I have painted views from the insect's perspective in the picture I showed you. Of course, the exterior designs of flowers are interesting, too. I have a collection of them here."

So saying, Kei took from the bookcase a bound volume of colored pictures.

"I didn't expect to be shown pornography," said Shō, opening this "custom-made picture book" on his lap.

"It's not as exciting as you might expect," said Kei. "I've manipulated them by computer graphics. Enlarged to this extent, human bodies and flowers become like abstract paintings. I have also changed the colors."

Shō was clearly impressed. "A very pleasing collection—it might not even be censored if you published it as an art book."

He asked Kei how he had managed to collect so many of them. Kei answered that he did it through his computer network.

"How does that work, precisely?"

"In short, I massage their brains. I keep sending messages to them to convince them that they are flowers. A sort of courtship, to use an old term. I then ask them to show their flowery parts. They send the images to the display. But fewer than ten girls have given me such presents. That's why I said I can't compete with you in terms of sheer numbers."

"Well, I cannot possibly equal you. But what do you give them in return?"

"Whatever they may want," Kei replied nonchalantly.

"For example?"

"Use your imagination."

"I'll let my imagination run wild, then. If I were a flower, I would like to receive an insect, melt it with the honey and devour it . . ."

"Not necessarily. Goddesses of flora are not as insectivorous as you might imagine. For example, some girls want to have my drawings of their parts. From ancient times, girls have loved to have pictures drawn of themselves. So I create flower abstractions from the print-out of the computer display. This usually pleases them most."

"And to please girls pleases you most, Kei."

"Exactly." Saying this, from the many completed paintings Kei selected one in delicate tones of lemon and pearl to show to Shō.

"Not bad. What kind of girl is this a picture of?"

"Well, since you're here, I would like you to take it back with you. It was requested by your elder sister Mai some time ago. I've just finished painting it."

"To my sister?" It took Shō a while to relax his face into a smile.

The Long Passage of Dreams

(Nagai yumeji (1968))

When Mariko arrived home, Keisaku's face had already changed into a face she did not know. Without uttering the word *Father,* she stood frozen at the foot of the sickbed. This was the first time she had seen the shadow of death. Though it resembled the mask of the *yaseotoko,* or "lovelorn man," worn by the protagonist, Lesser Captain Fukakusa, in *Courting Komachi,** the still-living face was in fact uglier. The lower jaw had dropped onto the chest, and the forced-open dark cavern of the mouth dominated the entire face. All one saw was the respirator. Compared to this outlandish gaping breathing hole, the face itself looked extremely small. It made one think of the neck mummies, shrunken to the size of fists, which they say are made by the savage tribes of the Amazon. What power must have been at work to change this face so completely? Mariko felt as though she had seen something in the shape of a black dog dragging her father between its teeth. That was the dream

---

*"Kayoi Komachi," a Noh play attributed to Kan'ami Kiyotsugu (1333–84). An entire translation of the play by Eileen Kato as "Komachi and the Hundred Nights" is included in Donald Keene, ed., *Twenty Plays of the Noh Theatre* (New York: Columbia University Press, 1970), 193–205. The excerpts from the play are, however, in my own translation.—trans.

she always had at times of sickness, but Mariko, having dreamt countless times of the black dog biting her father, toppling him, dragging him along, could not forget it. Could that black dog be Cerberus, out of Greek mythology? But the thing now by her father's pillow, grasping her father's face with its hand, despite being formless and invisible, was a far more distinct entity; it was death. It was no eerie black dog, no Cerberus—it was the horrible Thanatos. Mariko had always confused the Greek word for "death" with that for "time," *Chronos.* As if confusing twin brothers, she often imagined *death* to be Chronos and *time* Thanatos. Now both words floated before her eyes. The thing that had laid hold of Keisaku's face and transformed it into the shadow of death was the same whether one called it Death or Time. No one can obstruct the workings of that power; Mariko herself had kept aloof from the people who had been working to obstruct it. She left Time to his cruel work, to the decline that had transformed her father into something one would not think human, and spent these more than ten months with forced indifference. Now as Mariko tried to sit in this room, that fact pierced her like a lance, from pelvis to breast.

"Please address your father," Fusa said. As if dragged by these words, Mariko swung her knees down and brought her face close to her father's. His eyes were open and glistening but they still made her think of Himi's mask of the lovelorn man—the mask of a man from the realm of the dead, whose eyes were painted with gold dust. Then in a voice that wasn't a voice she said sharply, "Father!"

"Sis, you made it in time," said Masayo. Surprisingly Mariko, hearing this tearful voice, was better able to control her own emotions, which had been about to explode.

"I didn't think he would last until evening." It was

Keisaku's younger cousin, one of the many doctors in Keisaku's family, who said this. "He was definitely waiting for Mari-chan to get home."

Mariko accepted this hackneyed sentiment gently. The cousin went on to say in a physician's tone that they had tried everything; now there was nothing left to do but wait.

"You must be tired, Mari-chan," said her aunt. "How long does it take from New York to here?"

"It can take less than a whole day, at its fastest," Mariko said. "Of course you have to allow time for changing planes," she added. She felt a slight dizziness. Having flown in the opposite direction of the spinning earth, her sense of time was completely screwed up. When had she been walking across the Brooklyn Bridge? She couldn't tell. She had come to feel as if the Brooklyn Bridge was the same bridge that spanned the bay right outside the city.

On that bridge, Mariko was embracing a foreign man. Wound in her windswept hair, her face was like a ball rolling in straw. The man's arms were strong; he held her so close she could hardly breathe. The man's lips sought Mariko's through her hair.

The bridge resembled one of those dangerous footpaths made of narrow boards laid over the outer edges of a steel trestle, which country children loved to cross on their way home from school, although it's forbidden. Now that it had grown dark, it was not a place one should be walking. No matter how far they went, the bridge stretched ever farther. In the center of the bridge the lights of cars trailed off like spermatozoa. There was no one walking across the bridge besides Mariko and the man. The man holding Mariko as they walked was like a dark-faced messenger from the nether world. The water under the bridge, neither river nor sea nor lake, as far away as heaven is from earth, was a sheet of darkness like the skin of the beast that covers hell, and Mariko and the man seemed about to fall into it, entangled.

Wrapped in the man's arms, in a corner of her mind apart from her fear, Mariko thought about a novel. If she crossed this bridge safely, she could write about it in a novel. Writing novels was her work, so it was not unusual that there was another Mariko who should think soberly about novels at a time like this.

Mariko tried to remember what it was that could be put in a novel, but she was not confident of capturing it. It disappeared immediately, like a flimsy soap bubble. Why did she self-indulgently fill her mind with trivial thoughts like this in the middle of the ritual gathering around a human being nearing death? It was like doing obscene things to your body under your clothes, where no one can see. Knowing it was an attempt at self-distraction from the fact of her father's death, Mariko looked at her mother, as if in search of something that would suppress this capricious impulse.

Mother said, "Your kimono has been set out downstairs."

Mariko stood up, saying, "Yes," bowed to the people gathered in the room, and went into the hallway. A strange feeling as she trod across the straw matting drew Mariko's attention to her feet, which were feeling stuffy from wearing shoes for a long time. The nylon stockings she had worn all the way from the U.S. seemed like a tissue of dust veiling her feet.

She descended the stairway and, going into the bathroom, washed her feet with the light off. There was a new electric washing machine. The bathtub with no bottom was still there from the old days. But the cover was dry, and it was gathering dust; it seemed not to have been used in some time. Straining her eyes, she made out a spiderweb in the dim light. Had Mariko returned to a deserted house whose inhabitants had all passed away? Were the ones she had just been observing demons converted into human form? Suddenly a shadow blocked the doorway. It called out "Sis!" to Mariko, whose cry of surprise caught in her throat.

"What are you doing in here? If you're looking for the bathtub, a new one's been installed over there."

She replied weakly, "Oh, really?" and tried to calm herself. "I was washing my feet. Aren't those insect calls something?"

"There are a lot of insects in the back of the garden. Sometimes you can hear fruit crickets in a whole creaking orchestra. Even in the furnace of this bathtub there are crickets chirping."

Mariko faced the mirror stand to fix her hair.

"I'll help you," said Masayo, making her way around behind Mariko.

"What happened to the old mirror stand?"

"That one's in a corner of the sitting room. Mother uses it now and then. This one was bought for me—when I started learning Kabuki dancing."

Mariko remembered her younger sister saying she had been taking dance lessons two or three years earlier. Mariko tried her best not to concern herself with family affairs, including facts like that.

"My hair's filthy, isn't it"

Masayo said, "No it's not," and set about combing it. "Maybe because you haven't been taking good care of it, it looks stiffer than before."

To Mariko this seemed like a criticism of her lifestyle. Mariko hoped to hear the praise Masayo had often bestowed in the past.

As expected, Masayo said, "The nape of your neck is

long and clean, Sister. It really looks good in a kimono." She continued putting up Mariko's hair, a very serious expression on her face. The two sisters' faces were side by side in the mirror.

Unsmiling, Masayo said, "You've become thinner, Sister."

In the face of her chubby younger sister Mariko saw an excess of stifling youthfulness. The full cheeks made her eyes seem even narrower, and slightly turned up at the edges. If Masayo's face was *koomote* for a young woman's role, then Mariko's was a *rōjo* or *komachi* face for an aging woman's. Mariko glanced at the traces of emaciation around her own eyes as Masayo said "You're getting to look more and more like Mother." This too was something that Mariko had expected her to say.

Kōji came out of the kitchen. "Sister, have you had supper yet?" he asked.

"Come to think of it, I haven't eaten since Anchorage."

"If only Mother would eat too," Masayo said. "A body can't survive without eating."

"Still won't eat," Kōji said. When Kōji talked about his mother with outsiders, he called her "my mother," but within the family, he would avoid referring to her directly. Mariko had noticed this before. Her mother, who had shed hunger like a snake sheds its skin, always ate as if she were putting something unclean in her mouth. And Mariko could hardly remember the last time her mother had eaten anything even that way. Her mother had been sitting up straight as a candlestick at her father's bedside since morning.

"Go call Mother," Mariko said.

"He'll be okay for ten or fifteen minutes, don't you think," said Kōji, but without making a move to go up to the second floor. He motioned to his younger sister with his chin.

Their mother came downstairs. Mariko asked if the maid

was around. "I sent her home last night," Fusa replied, and sat down on her legs at the wide dining table above the large dugout brazier. Mariko sat down, her legs dangling. In the unlit *kotatsu* she felt the coolness of an autumn wind on her free bare legs as it had drifted in. With only Keisaku missing, the four family members began a simple dinner. Even when Keisaku was healthy, there were times when he was busy treating patients until nearly nine o'clock, so this had happened often. At those times, however, Fusa would sit at the table with the children, without eating. When Keisaku finished work, he would have a late supper and a late-night drink; she would sit in the same manner and wait on him. Mariko had often wondered when her mother would ever have dinner. Now, with her father's place empty, her mother was quietly eating. Among the things that Kōji, a skillful cook, had lined up and called "the twelve-dish traditional family *chazuke,*" Fusa touched neither the red miso soup with red snapper nor the scrambled eggs. But she did quickly eat two bowls of rice. It wasn't a manner of eating driven by hunger, nor did she make an unsightly display of consuming food as if it were distasteful; and it was far from the way animals eat. It was exactly like part of some ceremony; she didn't make a sound, and only the very tips of her chopsticks got the least bit dirty. In regard to dining, Keisaku, who was hard to please and concerned with manners above all else, was no rival for Fusa. He tended to slurp away, engrossed in his eating.

"Mr. Takatsu is here."

"Mr. Takatsu?" Mariko said, startled.

"The fall exams have just begun at the university, so he doesn't have classes. He's been showing up for a few days now."

"You didn't ask him to leave?"

"I'd like to have Mr. Takatsu see that man's last days," her mother replied in a hoarse, composed voice. "He does have that kind of relationship with us. Also, I thought that if by some chance you didn't return in time . . ."

Mariko sensed the frightening, more than cruel intent behind her mother's words, and her shoulders stiffened. The word *witch* floated again through her mind. Existing beyond the bounds of such things as psychological explanations, a witch was nothing other than a deep-rooted fantasy that over time had taken the fixed form of a mountain witch. In spite of any modern explanation that might be offered, this seemed to her just as plausible as the tales of how a mountain potato had changed into a mountain witch, or how a gate blown away by a typhoon had become a mountain witch.

"At any rate, it's good that you did make it in time," said her mother. "I'm sure he knows that you've come back; it's just that he doesn't have the strength to express it with his face."

"And if only the transfers had worked out more smoothly, I could have come even sooner," said Mariko. In the presence of her mother she could never speak but in excuses, and she was fully aware that they were never good enough.

When she had arrived at Haneda, as she walked along the passageway for transfers from international to domestic lines, Mariko had remembered the premonition she'd had before, that when the time came to walk breathlessly through this passageway, it would be when something bad had occurred. That inauspicious event could only be her father's death—she could not imagine any misfortune befalling her mother. Mariko firmly believed that her mother would never die of a disease—were she to die, it would be suicide. But why should a woman who had become alienated from humanity commit suicide? In that moment too, the notion of the "mountain witch" had floated through her mind.

That her father's condition might become critical at any moment she had gathered from her mother's overseas call to New York. Something similar had happened at the height of summer, but then she had let the impulse to return home pass. At that time, her father had still been able to speak.

In the lobby of Haneda Airport, Mariko had seriously considered stopping off somewhere on the way home, perhaps in Kyoto or Kobe. Her mind was still capable of something like that—the impulse to delay her return had entwined itself about her body like the sea serpents that crushed Laocoön to death. To preempt it, Mariko had made a long-distance call home. Kōji answered the phone, and told her that the doctors doubted whether their father would make it to nightfall. Resolutely saying, "I'll be home soon. Please tell Mother," Mariko had hung up. That was this afternoon.

Mariko had finished changing into her kimono and was about to go up the stairs when someone called her name. She turned to see Takatsu standing in the dim light of the hallway.

"Please forgive me," he said, lowering his head. She responded with a vague bow and stood there silently.

Takatsu's face showed no particular emotion. Mariko thought this was right. If it had been like the face that appears when you peel back a crab's shell, Mariko would never have forgiven such rudeness. Takatsu's face, with its blank expression, showed true courtesy. Mariko made a show of looking down upon him from on high. If they stood like this for a while, Mariko felt, her own face would set like plaster. She felt she had to do something. Couldn't she lift her hand and give him a graceful slap on the cheek? An act sanctioned by ceremony, this could not be considered a breach of decorum. Rather, toward Takatsu, who must gird himself in the mistaken concept of "responsibility" for having brought on her father's death, it would be an appropriate act, well suited to proper behavior.

On Mariko's part, however, there was a hesitation to touch Takatsu. A relationship had formed between the two of them that made it seem as if they could stroke the folds of each other's brains with tendrils of words. They were not in the habit of touching each other with hands or lips. Masayo described it as "a platonic but obscene relationship between Sister and Mr. Takatsu." Things had been left like that when Mariko went to spend some time in the United States, while Takatsu, who had just returned from Europe, had become an associate professor at a college.

In December of last year, while Mariko was away, Takatsu had come to her parents to ask them for permission to marry her. Keisaku had been delighted at the request, but Fusa had greeted him with that witchlike manner of hers, which usually prevented her from opening herself to others. Though she had no serious complaints about Takatsu as a person, she was unhappy with the suddenness of the request, many steps that she considered necessary having been omitted. The blame, as always, fell upon Mariko. Fusa kept repeating, "We never had a word about this from our daughter." Keisaku considered Mariko a "female rake," though he said this with a cheerful expression, as if toying with the ends of Mariko's long hair, which he seemed always to feel in his hand, however far away she might be. Moreover, he harbored trepidations about her being still single and facing thirty. But whenever Fusa would put these same trepidations into words, he would say "Let her do as she wants!" in a rather irritated tone. So Keisaku was delighted at Takatsu's visit, and as was the rule in such cases, he was not satisfied until he'd accompanied Takatsu to a riverside restaurant, in spite of a slight cold, and showered him with excessive hospitality. That had been the night of his first brain hemorrhage—Keisaku had tumbled into Takatsu's lap.

"What did Father reply?" Mariko asked, her hands dangling at her sides.

"He said, 'It depends on Mariko's feelings.' "

"That is not an answer."

"No?" said Takatsu, his face expressionless.

"I wanted to know how determined Father was. At such times I do not think that any response but 'Please take good care of my daughter' is a real response."

"Is that Mariko's desire?"

"That Father give you such an answer, yes. As for my response to you, Mr. Takatsu, I would consider it after that."

Mariko realized she was calling Takatsu by his family name, which hadn't been the case two years ago; she savored this new feeling.

When she went upstairs, neither her aunt nor the doctor was present; Mother was still sitting at the bedside like a candle holder. Mariko sat a short distance from her mother. The face of the sick man seemed yet one step closer to death. His fall away from the world Mariko and the others shared now seemed irreversible. From time to time his breathing grew agitated. It seemed as if his eyes were still open, veiled by a membrane, but that the pupils had rotated, and the eyes that once looked out were now facing inward, as if the moon had turned to reveal the far side that is normally hidden. Keisaku was gazing into the empty space within himself. The metallic eyes of the "lovelorn man" now turned on Mariko were ghostly, as if they were saying *I am finished with you all.*

In the letters he sent to Mariko in the States, Takatsu, drawing on the words of Heraclitus, observed that after becoming half paralyzed, Keisaku began to withdraw into his own world, like a bag gradually crumpling inward. Takatsu pointed out that this was a telltale sign that a person was close to death. Not even once did Mariko read back over those letters in Takatsu's upright handwriting, in language reminiscent of a mix of Montaigne and Alain. As a rule, they were like a well-mannered doctor's case history. Mariko understood why her father had opened his heart to this type of man but nonetheless felt a reluctance to acknowledge that the old man and the youth shared such a bond of sympathy. It infuriated her that Takatsu had covered over the growing fissure in her father, which opened inward, and that he had begun to fulfill the role of an intermediary between her father and the outside world—a role that Mariko felt should really have been hers. But Mariko understood that she could not have endured it. She grew as distant from her father as possible; she wished to be connected to him by only a sense of regret such as one would feel upon abandoning a helpless kitten.

"What time is it?" Masayo wondered aloud.

Kōji answered, "Coming up on seven." As Mariko thought to herself, Why is she asking the time? Kōji added "The low tide is at nine."

These words came to Mariko like a revelation, and the appointed time was engraved in her mind. How she would spend the roughly two hours till then, Mariko could not imagine.

She stood and went into the next room, where Takatsu

was sitting at the window with the lights off. This was the room Keisaku had lived in; in it were a simple writing table and rattan chairs and a leather armchair. In the alcove stood jars and vases in disarray; on top of the old lacquer sitting desk before it were an inkstone case, an iron kettle, a wooden box filled with tea utensils, and over a hundred songbooks bound in the Japanese style.

"What are you doing there?" said Mariko as she sat down before Takatsu. Between them was the writing desk, and on it one of the songbooks was lying open. Mariko half-consciously reached out and picked it up.

"Courting Komachi," she read aloud. Her eyes still downcast, she asked, "Has Father been practicing this in particular recently?"

"I don't really think so. I just opened the one that happened to be on top. Your father likes a great number, all sorts—it seems like whenever I'd mention a Noh play I'd seen in Tokyo, he'd say, 'That one's good; I like that one.' "

Mariko noticed that Takatsu's manner of speech was slightly more polite and formal than it used to be, and she thought it funny. It also seemed as if the proper way he sat at the desk was the result of some kind of training. She recalled a letter in which Takatsu had written that he was studying Noh dancing with the eldest son from the main house of the school her father had gone to; it was most likely her father who had made the arrangements.

That person had always come to relax in this area at the height of summer and would often spend several days at Mariko's house. Mariko had run into him two or three times during summer vacations in her college days. Among other things, they had once gone to the movies together. Mariko had been dumbfounded by the courtesy of his demeanor and the politeness of his speech. That was when she had first given any attention to the terms *politesse* and *grâce.* Afterward, Mariko recognized that she had felt daunted and was embarrassed that she had not worn makeup. Takatsu's mannerisms had in some way come to resemble that person's.

"When *Courting Komachi* and *Stupa of Komachi* came up, your father said that just like Lesser Captain Fukakusa, he too had gone back and forth one hundred nights."

"To my mother's place?"

"You should know."

"Well, one hundred nights is an exaggeration," Mariko said, laughing, "but I wonder, when my father made the trip on a hundred nights, did he score the number of times into his shaft bench?"

"What he did was write a hundred love letters," Takatsu said with a serious expression.

"That can't be true."

"You've hardly ever spoken about your father and mother, Mariko. Perhaps there are things I know more about than you do."

At the time her father was in Tokyo, a student at a school of dentistry. Mariko knew her mother had come to Tokyo from an old family in Kumano, to stay with her aunt and pass the days taking lessons in the arts. It seems that her father had a crush on her mother around this time, but Mariko didn't know in detail how her father had played the role of Lesser Captain Fukakusa.

> *Komachi:* I never imagined such obsession would await me in the next life.
>
> *Fukakusa:* She promised me her love if I would visit the shaft bench of her carriage, on one hundred nights. And I believed her! Night after night, I would get on the carriage and sneak my way to the shaft bench just before dawn.

Komachi: I forbade him to come by carriage, lest he draw attention, and told him to come in disguise.

Fukakusa: So I couldn't use my palanquin or carriage.

Komachi: Though I expected his love would cease someday.

Chorus: He could have hired a horse in Kowata Village, in Yamashiro.

Fukakusa: But I walked barefoot out of passion for you.

Komachi: And you were dressed in?

Fukakusa: A straw hat and coat.

Komachi: A bamboo cane with as many knots as troubles in human lives.

Fukakusa: By moonlight the road was not that dark.

Komachi: And on snowy nights?

Fukakusa: I brushed snowflakes off my sleeves.

Komachi: And when it rained?

Fukakusa: I dreaded invisible demons who might devour me in one gulp.

Komachi: And if it happened to be cloudless?

Fukakusa: Still a rain of tears fell on me alone. Ah, what a dark night!

Mariko read this, mouthing the words.

"I heard that your parents met at the Noh Theater in Yotsuya, didn't they?"

"When my mother was young, I think she learned a little bit of Noh chanting and dancing. She was taller than the women of old, and I'm told she studied it to improve her posture."

"It was to see your mother that your father started studying it."

"That's the first I've heard of it."

"Not long after that your mother stopped going. Then your father ended up commuting every night from Jinbō-chō to Sanban-chō. Late at night, while everyone in her aunt's house was sound asleep—of course, your mother was sleeping too—he would drop a letter in their mailbox. Your mother, the first one up in the morning, would slip it into her sleeve and go back inside."

"If that's true," Mariko said, struggling with an uncomfortable sensation akin to jealousy, "what did Father think of to write on those hundred visits, I wonder."

"He joked to me that in the end he had nothing left to write, so he just noted the number of visits and kept writing the same phrase."

The first time he lost control of his bladder, Keisaku was sitting out on a couch in the sunny second-floor hallway, bundled up in a blanket. Beyond the glass doors the wind was howling, but in the space between the translucent paper sliding doors of the living room and the outer glass doors, the winter sunlight collected like lukewarm water. Suddenly this chamber grew dark. Before he'd had time to wonder whether it was a bank of wind-driven clouds scudding across the sky that had hidden the sun, Keisaku slumped—it felt as if his left side were immersed in a wintry lake. The fact that he could not lift his arms and that his field of vision had suddenly shrunk clearly meant something out of the ordinary had occurred. Before he knew it, Keisaku was wearing one of Himi's masks. The mask had become the skin of his face and was firmly affixed there, and Keisaku could now see his own face from the inside. It was the face of an old man, the shadow of death frozen upon it. In this guise of the "lovelorn man" Keisaku stood up and touched the sliding paper door. Inside this room with its north-facing window the chill of the spirit world was overflowing. As it became like an ice-house, Keisaku called out to Fusa, who he thought was inside.

"The northern window seems to be open. Come close it."

Hearing no answer, Keisaku opened the sliding doors. A young Fusa was sitting there.

"What are you doing in here?"

"Since you pursue me, I'll no longer go out on the path where the sun shines."

"I pursue you only because you told me to come a hundred times bringing love letters. I'm not a mailman," Keisaku said in an irritated manner, though he thought it all absurd. "Lie if you must, but how about giving me an answer, once and for all?"

"If a lie will do, that I'll give you," Fusa said cheerfully, eyebrows raised. "I'll be all yours. But you must come a hundred nights."

"I don't have that kind of time anymore. I'm beginning to die."

"You are dead." With this Fusa stood up and bumped Keisaku's chest with her shoulder; then she turned and ran away. On a piece of paper that fluttered behind her fleeing white *tabi* he read the words: *Returning to Kumano.* That was what had happened on the ninety-ninth night. Keisaku ran, gasping, toward some train station. As he ran, he thought about the many taxicabs he could have taken that would be drifting over the city like luminescent bugs if it had been now. And he thought that if he did it now, he could fly to Osaka and arrive ahead of Fusa and wait for her. He became so impatient that he felt as if his throat were scorched. But Keisaku knew the city street that he was running along was the street of forty years ago. The houses were low, and the scene was dim as the image on a sooty poster. He saw an unmanned rickshaw sitting, on a deserted street corner, its shafts pointing skyward. Though he knew it was silly, he began pulling the rickshaw as he ran.

He arrived at the station and dashed up the stairs, out of breath. A train seemed just to have left. Keisaku sat down, and in his mind he heard the voice of a narrator intone, "He was to make his visit on a hundred nights. On the ninety-ninth night he suffered from an oppressive dizziness and a heavy feeling in his chest. Before that night was done, he died, Lesser Captain Fukakusa. . . .* It's not supposed to go this way, Keisaku thought, trying to search the well of his memory. But in his crippled brain, even the location of that well seemed lost beneath a mass of rubble. Keisaku thought that he had caught Fusa then. But "now" was "then."

As he had expected, Fusa was there. She was sitting wrapped in a shawl on a bench on the tip of the platform, like abandoned luggage. When he went closer, it was a girl with a small, white, egg-shaped face who appeared out of the darkness and greeted Keisaku.

"I thought you'd come," Fusa said, letting out a deep breath.

"I won't let you go again. I'm going along to Kumano with you," Keisaku said like an impulsive youth, but the voice that came out was that of an old man, his face the death mask of the "lovelorn man." As he thought that it would be better if Fusa didn't notice, behind the mask of his age and ugliness he felt unfurling the wings of a licentious desire. The girl's face was as youthful as the *koomote* mask—a little different from the face of Fusa back then. Keisaku imagined raping this girl with his old body and felt a brutal joy near madness.

---

*A quote from a Noh play, *Sotoba Komachi* (*The Stupa of Komachi*), in my translation. An entire translation of this play, which is attributed to Kanze Motokiyo, is entitled *Komachi on the Gravepost* and included in Royal Tyler, trans., *Granny Mountains: A Cycle of Nō Plays* (Ithaca: Cornell China–Japan Program, 1978), 105–16.—trans.

"Your ticket is bought already," the girl said, and opening her fist, she showed it to him. He took her hand and pulled her close, and drawn to him as if weightless, the girl dropped her head against his chest. Though mindful of his old man's breath, Keisaku thought of seeking her lips. But none of this had happened forty years ago. Bewildered by that vague doubt, Keisaku continued to stroke the girl's cold hair, made damp by the fog. In his hands the hair took on a terrible silver sheen. The face looking up at him was now a demon's mask—a *shinja* or "true snake" mask with protruding tongue.

From the stir of Fusa's movements near his feet, Keisaku knew he had urinated.

Letting his anger get the best of him, he said, "How long is it you've been a true snake?"

Keisaku intentionally mumbled, and the question came out a virtually inaudible groan. Even Fusa, long accustomed to deciphering Keisaku's indistinct speech, found it incomprehensible.

Looking into Keisaku's face, Fusa asked, "Did you say something?" Keisaku gave another groan of displeasure, signifying "never mind."

As his sickness worsened and his tongue ceased to function, Keisaku began deliberately mumbling his words. Then with hate-filled eyes, he would doggedly refuse to accept that his family, who could not make heads or tails of what he'd said, were so confused they could do nothing but stare at him quizzically. At such times a person's face looks extremely foolish. Even Fusa, whose face seldom had any expression, was not exempt. He was able to despise Fusa, with her foolish deaf face, to his heart's content. At times like this Keisaku would grind his teeth with abhorrence, with anger at Fusa and at himself, who had stooped so low.

Fusa, however, soon saw through this trick, and came to nonchalantly disregard any particularly indistinct words. His helpless rage at Fusa, who calmly tried to control him as an unseemly, foolish, and half-paralyzed invalid, had bordered on the infantile. By and by, Keisaku abandoned his assault, and grew accustomed to the fact that he must meekly entrust his body to her care, like an infant. Still, when Fusa unconcernedly said things like, "Would you please speak more clearly," he was instantly beside himself with indignation. Keisaku tried to explain, "I am not doing this because I want to, but because I can no longer speak any other way" but stopped short. Tears clouded over the sick man's muddy eyes.

A short time earlier, around the time Keisaku had stabilized after his first collapse, Mariko had been in Iowa and had heard his voice via an international phone call. It was Fusa who made the call, but she quickly handed the phone to Keisaku. Her father had made an effort to sound cheerful, trying to conceal his newly acquired lisp. Sympathy surged through her, and she felt the blood rush from her face.

"My left side has become a little numb and my tongue lisps a bit. You can't tell when I chant Noh songs, but when I'm talking to people, I sometimes can't hide it. So I've gradually come to dislike people altogether. Are you all right?"

"Yes. I'm planning to return as soon as I can."

"Take your time. Enjoy yourself."

"Please don't overexert yourself, especially when it's cold. We don't want your blood pressure rising."

"I'm fine. What's more important is you—you sound a little down; you're not your usual self. Are you in poor health or something?"

"No. But it's extremely cold here. It's below sixteen degrees outside—it seems like even one's voice is going to freeze."

Looking back on that now, though, Mariko thought to herself, Then, the flowers still remained on the withering tree. She had not thought her father would continue growing weaker, steadily sinking into the pit of death as if walking down a slope—or rather she had tried not to think that. Even if this were to happen, it struck her as something to be viewed as a remote contingency and filed away in the depths of a drawer not normally opened. Since then the flow of time had seemed something like a bad dream to her—both long and short. Only regret now remained, as on those mornings when only the fatigue of dreams lingers after the sleeper awakes.

"When I saw Father this time I was surprised at how much his face had changed," Mariko said to Takatsu. "This time he's definitely leaving us, isn't he?"

"He's changed a lot, even just today."

"I saw immediately that the glow had left his cheeks completely. His face is like a rotting log that's fallen to earth. No, not like a log—that's just a plant. It's an ugly thing I can't bear to look at." As she said this, Mariko became agitated; she fixed her gaze on one spot, power filling her crushed voice. "I can't watch. I can't possibly look on until the end."

"But you've got to be there and watch over him," Takatsu said. He stood up and looked out the window at the featureless dark outside. "Your father may be well aware you've come home. He can't communicate that to us because he can't move his mouth or his eyes, but his brain may still be living and working. He may be thinking just for himself . . . without words anymore."

"Without words anymore?" Mariko repeated in a tone like the muttering of a dreamer.

"Because he's fallen out of the shared world into the abyss of himself."

If that were so, she supposed, there was no way for anyone on the outside to glimpse the flickering fireworks of thought in her father's head. Mariko stood, mumbling, "Except by words . . ." As she lurched to her feet she rested her hand on Takatsu's shoulder.

"What time do you suppose it is?"

"It's a little before eight."

Someone called Mariko from the next room. For a moment she thought it was her father's voice she'd heard, and she replied in a voice she could not believe was her own.

Masayo was home for the summer, but Keisaku would often call her Mariko by mistake. Though he rarely did so in her presence, he hardly ever called her anything but Mariko, when no one was around. Perhaps it had become harder for him to admit the fact that Mariko was still in the U.S., and that Masayo was the one who was home for summer vacation. Whenever relatives paid their visits, Fusa would lament that Keisaku's mental ability had declined and tell them that Keisaku would speak deliriously at times and that he was no longer able to tell dreams from reality.

Keisaku did know, however, that Masayo was the one at home, not Mariko. Further, it was his own business to call "Mariko" as he wanted to. It was not easy to pronounce the name; his tongue felt not like something grown inside his mouth, but like a foreign object inserted from outside. Since he had already overcome the irritation with inability to utter words as he would want to, he would call "Mariko" now and again when no one was around, just to practice. It did not sound like any human's voice, but rather like the eerie groan of an animal. It sounded to him like a type of incantation. If it was one, then it might bring Mariko back with its magical power. But it was always Masayo or Fusa who would appear his side. As Masayo looked into his face, Keisaku would remain quiet. If she persisted in talking to him, he would turn away and look toward the window. "Father didn't seem to have wanted me," Masayo would complain to Fusa. Keisaku even knew that.

The locusts were very noisy in the back yard; with so many fruit trees, the yard was filled with their shrieking. It sounded as if they were being scorched by the burning heat of August. This reminded Keisaku of the haiku—"Locusts make one feel hot—the extent that I feel like cutting down the pine they are on."*

To look at it another way, locusts sounded like the passing rain pouring down on him, which made him think that perhaps one could say "Locusts make one feel cool." He was too weak to feel the summer heat as heat. From deep down inside, from the marrow of his bones, a sense of coolness spread throughout his body. And as his fever rose, this sense of coolness also intensified. The third time he experienced an attack was when the new tea leaves began to be distributed, and ever since he had been unable to get up or move by himself, mostly remaining stiff in bed. Eventually, the coolness oozed from the marrow of his bones through his skin, flowing out like water. The body like a deteriorated and fallen tree sank half in the middle of that cold water and passed day in and day out.

Keisaku made up his mind that it would be time to go on

---

*The original poem, by Yokoi Yayū (1787–1823) reads, "semi atsushi/ matsu kirabaya to/ omou made." Included in his "Semi (no) in" (1759).—trans.

a trip when the midsummer heat had passed and those cicadas had returned to the earth. This was nothing as grave as the anticipation of and preparation for his own death; it was just that the season when the sun weakened and the autumn wind began to rise seemed suitable for departure. Keisaku thought that Mariko must have come home at that time, and that she might see him off as far as the area of the riverside full of stones. Going with Mariko would also be fine. He must purchase two plane tickets and make plans before it was too late. The destination was the old capital. For Keisaku, it was a dream that seemed to float on a sea of clouds. He couldn't help but remember a sentence from *The Account of Living in a One-Foot-Square Room:* "The old capital was already destroyed, and the new one was yet to be built."* When he brought it to mind, a deep sense of having lived in bad times dogged him; this became resentment and righteous indignation worthy of an old man at the trend toward worldly customs. He was strangely off guard with Takatsu and often let that out. It would be okay if Takatsu joined them on the trip, Keisaku thought. In his mind Takatsu and Mariko were already husband and wife.

Before leaving on this trip, he'd have to set his hand to the ruined garden. He had carelessly planted the fruit trees too thickly, and it looked like it'd be better to uproot and dispose of some of them. As this thought came to his mind, Keisaku felt as if he had risen without trouble from his bed and was looking down at the back yard from the window. In the garden, persimmons, figs, loquats, pomegranates, citrons, orange trees and a number of other fruit trees were

---

*A quote from *Hōjōki* in my translation. Helen McCullough has translated the entire work as "An Account of My Hermitage" in her *Classical Japanese Prose: An Anthology* (Stanford: Stanford University Press, 1990), 379–92.—trans.

arranged haphazardly. When he had planted them, Fusa had objected, saying flowering shrubs would be better.

"Fruit-bearing trees are less graceful—besides, one must always worry about children climbing them to pick the fruit and falling and hurting themselves."

But Keisaku ignored her objections. He could not forget that during his childhood in the country, he himself had climbed innumerable fruit trees, greedily devouring the fruit while still perched in their branches.

Now the loquats were already gone, and it was too early yet to eat the fall fruits. Under the persimmon tree, the elementary-school pupil Mariko and three-year-old Kōji were hunched down, playing in the dirt. The small of Mariko's back peeked out from the space between her skirt and shirt. The children were digging something up. Keisaku leaned out of the second-story window and shouted to them in a loud voice.

"Hey, don't dig up the extracted teeth!"

To the children, "extracted teeth" was a strange expression. Moreover, the day they buried Keisaku's patients' extracted teeth was still in the future. Beneath the spot where the young Mariko was digging this time was supposed to be an air-raid shelter. So Keisaku corrected himself. "Don't play on top of the air-raid shelter!" he shouted.

At this, Mariko and Kōji looked up at the second-story window. These two faces, smeared with mud, had no noses or eyes. Keisaku, flustered, said, "Look at you! It's from playing in a place like that that your faces get that way."

"Father, we dug a hole," said a suddenly grown-up Mariko. On her forehead were smears of dirt, as if she'd wiped away sweat with the mud-covered back of her hand.

"Is that so? Good job. Leave one box for Kōji to practice his craft, and let's bury the rest."

There were apple boxes filled with what looked like kernels of corn—these were in fact extracted teeth pulled from the mouths of some tens of thousands of people. They made a dry rattling noise as the box was tilted and they were poured into the hole.

"Father, do you know the story about the teeth of the dragon slain by Cadmus?" asked Mariko.

"No, I don't."

"It's one of the Theban legends of ancient Greece. It's about how a hero named Cadmus defeated a dragon and then plowed the land of Thebes and sowed it with the dragon's teeth. Soon warriors in armor and helmets appeared from the ground and immediately began slaughtering each other."

"Is that so?" said Keisaku, who picked up a handful of teeth and sprinkled them over the yard, performing the movements of the *Setsubun* bean-scattering ceremony.

Mariko laughed. "That won't work—you have to plow properly and then plant them," she said, and then went on with her story. "These teeth of Cadmus also appear in the odyssey of the Argonauts. When Jason goes to the land of Colchis to get the golden fleece, the king of Colchis makes unreasonable demands on him: he is to plow the sacred grounds of Ares with a fire-breathing ox and then sow the teeth of Cadmus there. But because the princess Medea falls completely in love with Jason, he is able to manage it all quite well and succeeds in obtaining the golden fleece. Medea betrays her father and, leaving her family behind, decides to follow Jason."

"It seems like I've heard that story somewhere before."

"Quite likely," said Mariko with an enigmatic smile. "After all, Medea lives in this house."

"What does that mean?"

"Medea was a woman endowed at birth with magical powers. With her powers she saved Jason, but though she had abandoned her parents and siblings to follow him, Jason later contemplated a political marriage with another woman. Medea brooded over this and finally gave that princess a dress steeped in deadly poison; when the princess put it on she broke out in burning sores and died. Medea became a witch, even killing her own two children, and vanished into the air which bore her about." Keisaku thought of the woman in the Noh play *The Iron Ring,* whose face is the mask *hashihime* or Goddess at the Bridge. Keisaku had never worn this mask, but years before at a regular meeting he had performed the major role in the latter half of the play.

"'I will kill her now!' Then she brandishes her scourge above her rival's head, coils her hair about her hand, and strikes! In this sorrowful world, where we cannot tell what is real from what is not . . ."* Dancing to this passage, he had been told, Keisaku had represented the woman's passion quite well. Fusa was not like the *hashihime* of *The Iron Ring.*

"That means that woman called Medea turned into 'an invisible demon.' But I haven't done anything like that Greek man, whatever his name was. And I haven't done anything like the man in *The Iron Ring.* So why has she become a demon?"

"It's because you haven't treated her as one should treat Medea. You just stole her away from Kumano and did nothing for her."

"You're a woman—the older you become, the more you take your mother's part."

---

*A quote from "Kanawa," in my translation. See p. 59 for more information on the play.—trans.

"That's not true. It's you and I who are birds of a feather—you know that!" Mariko said, pouting. Her face then was just like Fusa's when she was young.

Keisaku followed that face as if following the moon passing through a dark sky. He dashed into Tokyo Station and seized Fusa. Inside the train, Fusa was as docile as a beast injured and caught by a hunter. Her body and mind had grown soft, and she seemed completely submissive to Keisaku's will. From that moment Keisaku forgot this woman's savageness and took it for granted that she would be easy to manage. The beast had not lost her talons or fangs, though—she only hid them within her soft fur and flesh. However, unlike Medea, she did not use them. Perhaps it was because Keisaku was not capable of a betrayal such as Jason's, but Fusa's magical powers were buried and instead raked her own body, like a lion's overgrown claws. And Keisaku thought that Fusa, corrupted by her own poison, had become like a witch in the guise of a faultless wife and mother.

On the train to Osaka, Keisaku asked about the hundred letters, and Fusa responded, "I ate them all." With eyes both bantering and seductive she returned Keisaku's gaze, chuckling. Such a look was typical of the Fusa of that time. She seemed with age to have acquired the skill of saying the most outrageous things in a mocking and sarcastic tone, leaving Keisaku with nothing tangible to find fault with. He detested the hardness of her heart but did not have the skills to fight her. He resumed his training in Noh chanting and dance, to have her less before him. As she reached the verge of womanhood, Mariko would laugh at Keisaku's evasiveness, and he felt like confessing to her something that might inoculate this gentle girl.

One day he said, "My marriage to your mother was a

mistake. At least on my part it was hopelessly misguided. At that time I was utterly in love with her, and as I look back on it, I see that I was filled then with a strange eagerness toward life. When I had some chance of opening my own business, I went to Kumano to ask for your mother's hand. However, as it came out it was more like a raid on their house, and I brought your mother home with me by outright robbery. Her family was unanimously against our marriage; her eldest brother, who had come to take the place of her father in the family, referred to me as a nobody and an immature youth. It turned into a real fight. Your mother finally said she meant to marry me even if it meant forsaking her own family, and so it was settled. In the end your mother was disowned, and she came to my home penniless and alone. I was deeply moved at the time by your mother's courage, but it remained a mystery to me how she was able to summon such resolve."

"Mother is strong enough to do it," Mariko said, her face hardening. "And she loved you then."

"No, it was nothing as simple as that. Your mother has never even once said that she loved me. She is a woman who can never tell a lie—her not saying that means that she felt nothing for me at all. What I didn't realize at the time was that her decision to give herself to the man who pursued her long enough was a matter that concerned her alone—it had nothing to do with any goodwill or sympathy toward me. But once made, her decision was absolutely irrevocable. That kind of strength is frightening. After I'd pulled off my theft, I got my stolen bride safely onto a ship out of Osaka, but from that time I began to feel a terror of her. At night, as the ship made its way I knew not where through the dark water, I began to realize that this thing I had pursued and finally had in my hands was nothing like what I had imagined, and as I thought about my prospects for the future, I grew more and more uneasy. But your mother sat calmly in the saloon, doing her knitting and whatnot. Like this Greek witch that you tell me of—and since that time I have been sure that she is not a woman either."

Shortly after he'd begun practicing Noh chanting again, he was puzzled by the expression "in one gulp, the demon devoured," which appears often in plays about devils and beasts, so he researched it and found the expression in the sixth story of *Tales of Ise.* "Once upon a time, there was a man who spent years wooing a woman he had no hope of winning. At last he went out and managed to steal her and ran away with her under cover of night." Later, not knowing that a demon lived there, they took refuge in a cellar during a rainstorm, and "the demon devoured her in one gulp."* She screamed out for help, but just then there was a crash of thunder, and the sound of her cry did not reach the man. Keisaku felt as if he were the man in the story. The only difference was that after eating her the demon had assumed the shape of the woman, so as to follow him around for ever after.

As Keisaku was thinking of telling this story to Mariko, he noticed that she seemed to be glaring at him, but with eyes that brimmed with tears. Enigmatic tears. He suddenly realized that he should not draw Mariko too close to himself. Sullenly, as if he were trying to push aside a hand grasping his, he said, "I've talked too much. Forget it. It's late, why don't you go on to sleep."

Mariko's eyes grew wide, and she stared at him with a

---

*A quote from *Ise monogatari* in my translation. For an entire translation of this episode, see Helen McCullough, trans., *The Tales of Ise* (Stanford: Stanford University Press, 1968), 72–73.—trans.

look of spite. As she left the room she said, bitingly, "I don't expect I'll be *able* to sleep tonight."

Keisaku, maintaining an impassive expression, mused to himself, "Because she's a demon's daughter too."

Something had happened around the time Mariko was born. Keisaku had a nightmare in which his child was born in the form of a bird's egg a foot across. But it was different from an egg with a shell; it was flesh, wrapped up in a kind of semitransparent membrane made of egg white. When this saclike thing was cut away, what emerged had neither head nor hands nor feet. There was only something shaped like the vaginal opening of a mature woman. Then the sky suddenly clouded over and an ominous bird flew down, grabbed the flesh egg, and flew away.

Keisaku made a note in his diary about this dream. At the end he added a sentence relating how Fusa, who had given birth to the egglike thing, grinned like a cat, but in fact this hadn't happened in the dream. Keisaku used to keep the diary in a bookcase with French doors that could be locked. But he often forgot to lock them, or left the book on his desk, so there was a good possibility that a family member had stolen a look at it. It would have been absurd to suspect Fusa; she wouldn't have read it even if she'd found it lying open on the desk. It was true she had opened and read letters to Mariko, as she thought she was entitled to do. But that was different. And once she'd had a heated argument with Mariko about a letter from a male friend, and Mariko, in tears, had asked her not to open letters like that anymore. From that time on Fusa had never touched a letter addressed to her. There was no one other than Mariko who would take advantage of an opportunity to peek at Keisaku's diary. Unlike Fusa, Mariko was dishonest—Keisaku could tell she was the kind of woman who could lie without difficulty. He would say this was one of Mariko's likable traits, but at some point even Keisaku was no longer able to tell when Mariko was lying. But this was a different kind of fear from that engendered by Fusa, who could never say anything that wasn't true.

"You read my diary, didn't you?" and "Have you slept with a man?" were two questions the answers to which Keisaku had thought he would like to hear from Mariko's mouth before he died. However, in the case of the latter question, time made it unnecessary. When Mariko passed twenty, Keisaku began to assume that she was sexually experienced, but, rather than basing this on his observation of her, he instead inferred it from his understanding of women of a given age. But in place of this question, now moot, he would have liked to ask something else: whether Mariko had given her body to Takatsu. Keisaku's intuition told him that the answer was no. Strangely flustered, Keisaku thought to himself, So this is what is meant by "a woman's heart cannot be known."

As far as the first question was concerned, Keisaku had sought out an answer for himself and gradually grew more convinced it was the right one—she had definitely been reading the diary. A subtle change in her demeanor since just before he had spoken to her of his marriage had convinced him of that. Before, her eyes had been the eyes of a daughter looking at her father—her vision had stopped at the "father mask" Keisaku wore; but at some point it had come to extend boldly inward, entering deep within his eyes, like a fishing line dropped to probe their depths. It was the kind of vision a woman who loves and who knows she is loved in return directs at her lover. Mariko could look at him that way because she knew she was known by him. For Mariko, Keisaku's dream that she was born in that egg of flesh was a revelation. It was to this dream birth that she now traced the beginning of her own existence, and it was none other than Keisaku who had borne her, by giving birth to this dream. Because of this it was Keisaku who knew Mariko's secrets. And once she knew she was known, wasn't it only natural that her eyes when looking at that man should become those of a completely known woman? This was how Keisaku made sense of it. And in the small leather-bound notebook he used as a diary, he wrote that down too.

He would take this diary with him on his trip with Mariko, thought Keisaku. In a Greek tragedy Mariko had once told him about, there was a king who had plucked out his own eyes and became a beggar, wandering the world in the care of his daughter—but would Mariko be so kind as to become his support? He couldn't really expect that kind of thing, Keisaku thought. Mariko had a strangely unfeeling streak. Or perhaps for Mariko, who always strove to distance herself from people, this was rather her essence. Compared to people like Fusa, who did not allow others to come close even while living in the midst of family, people like Mariko who abandoned and fled from people yet could barely be said to live, were quite cowardly, Keisaku thought to himself.

At some point the sun had set and an enormous, hemorrhaged, distorted moon appeared through the window. Keisaku knew that Mariko's plane would land soon.

Mariko went downstairs and put on the wristwatch she had left on the kitchen table. It was eight thirty. The gathering on the second floor had grown; her cousin Kō, who was three months older than Mariko, had joined it. Until their mid teens they had been so close that they were thought of as a pair, but Mariko had at some point distanced herself from him. He worked for some company in Tokyo and had taken a leave of absence and flown home. Ever since a certain age, Kō had begun to manifest a vulgarity and a tendency to try to control others, which drove Mariko from him. In spite of the fact that these aspects of his personality seemed more dominant, Mariko, on seeing him, felt a sense of nostalgia, as if she were running her hand over an old kimono. That hadn't happened when she saw Takatsu.

"Mari-chan, I understand this time Uncle is really bad," said Kō, his head bent as he took off his shoes. And, stiffly, as one sees in those who work in companies, with movements that appear to have been assimilated into a routine, he went upstairs. From the bottom of the staircase Mariko at last said, "Kō-chan, thanks for taking the trouble to come."

Masayo came down from the second floor, grasped Mariko's hand and pressed her head against Mariko's chest.

"Sister, I'm scared."

Her face having grown pale, Mariko shook Masayo off and went upstairs.

Her father was still breathing. She sat down next to her mother, cradling both a sense of relief and the uneasy feeling that she had been sentenced to endless postponements. Like her father's breathing, which had grown irregular, this was surely a sign of the ebbing tide. Mariko thought about what would depart along with this tide. If it were the spirit, then the thing left after the tide had gone out would be the vessel that had contained the spirit. She remembered that someone had once said that although living things are no more than matter, dead things are nothing but spirit or soul. One should rather say that while living things are spirits trapped in matter, the dead are only spirits liberated from their containers of flesh. Death was nothing but the separation of the spirit from matter. Would a dying person fear this liberation? Mariko was sure that her father would not. If the spirit endured hardships, these resulted from its attachment to the body. Of course this was nothing more than illusion, but that did not mean that it was easy for the spirit to reject this illusion. To avoid the fear of death, it was surely necessary for the spirit to practice rejecting everything in advance. And had her father not been doing just this kind of practice?

Mariko could not recall hearing her father speak of death. Once when he had brought up the death of his own father, he had said, "Be careful not to die that way." Mariko could not remember her grandfather's face. He had died when she was seven, and his last words, spoken as he was collapsing, were "I've made a mistake!" He had died suddenly of a heart attack. Preparations for his death had not been made—he had been expected to continue living. It was thus as if he'd been walking on the road and had suddenly fallen into a bottomless pit. In Keisaku's view, that was the least acceptable way to die. He was thinking more than anything of the confusion and inconvenience caused to survivors. Keisaku had also told her, "Since I am fearful by nature, I have seen to it that you will be able to make ends meet." However, even supposing he was completely prepared in terms of these secular concerns, what kind of preparations had he made for the inevitable fall into his own pit? Mariko knew almost nothing about what shape her father's spirit (after he quit his dental practice) might have taken in that swiftly decaying receptacle. According to Takatsu's letter, Keisaku's decision to retire had been completely unexpected. Fusa and Keisaku's siblings had assumed that

Keisaku would not close his office at least until such time as Kōji should qualify as a dentist and succeed him. But on New Year's Eve the year before last year, Keisaku told Fusa, "I'll quit my practice starting next year." In a letter Takatsu had said that Keisaku was persistent. When relatives on a New Year's visit urged him to change his mind, he refused, saying, "I do not have confidence in my body any longer. Accordingly, I have no confidence in my skills."

His actual motives, however, as he later revealed to Takatsu, had been slightly different.

"In short, I've reached the point where I've come to hate it. When I was a kid, I hung out with various crowds; there were times when it suddenly occurred to me I'd had enough of them. At such times, I promptly dropped them all together, having told myself, 'I'll stop; I'm sick of this.' Since growing up, I've never done that. I've long grown tired of repairing the insides of people's mouths. I've been fed up with it, let me see . . . for forty years. It's just one of those jobs one could only do because of the need to earn a living. It's impossible to fall in love with it. It requires endurance—just bearing up and getting the job done. I began to dream at one point that someday I'd tell myself, 'I've come to hate this. I'm quitting, damn it—I'll leave this job and go on.' I endured only by looking forward to this. Now that I come to think about it, isn't it pitiful that I went on living, knowing that my essential being was not in it? I endured, thinking it was all just a temporary 'me'—then when I tried to return to the real me, I couldn't figure out where the real me had gone. Honestly, I am tired of this game too. I almost want to leave this world all together, to say 'I'm quitting. I'm tired of it.'"

Lying on his back staring at the ceiling, Keisaku tried to call Mariko with his willpower. The airplane Mariko was on was flying low, its wings buzzing like a gadfly—before long it would appear in the back yard. I've got to leave the window open, Keisaku thought. Just as he did so, the window opened. The dry autumn air filled the room. With a roaring sound, the airplane came into the room through the open window and landed above Keisaku's face. It was like looking up at a ship at anchor from the bottom of the sea. The fuselage was like a fish's body, its belly red, its sides sparkling silver. The belly split open and a ladder came out, and in a short time Mariko was standing at his bedside. She was wearing something like a rubber diving suit.

"Why are you wearing that? Take it off immediately." As soon as Keisaku had said this, Mariko reached around behind her and immediately stripped it off and threw it at her feet. Underneath the suit she was naked.

"Did you want something from me?"

"I got sick, so I called you back."

"You wanted to call me back, so you got sick."

"My thoughts have gotten more perverse, and my brain has started to rot."

"I understand every nook and cranny of your thoughts, Father. Ever since you let me read your diary."

"So you did read it, on the sly."

"The person who purposely left it open on the table for me to read was you, Father."

"Well then there's no need for an explanation now. I'm taking you on a trip with me."

"You can't do that in your condition."

"There's nothing to worry about. Actually, this is just a feigned illness. Are you mad?"

"Yes, I am," Mariko said, laughing. She yawned like a cat. Her fangs and rough tongue glistened. "If you want to go on a trip with me that badly, then carry me on your back."

Don't try that trick on me—before I've gone a mile this girl intends to change into a horrible demon and eat me in one gulp, Keisaku thought to himself. "I'm not that strong," he said. "I'm a blind beggar. You take my hand and lead me."

"Like King Oedipus and Antigone . . ."

"No, I am Akushich-byōe Kagekiyo." Saying this, Keisaku found himself in a straw hut, chanting: "Indeed, there is no place to settle in the Three Worlds of Being. Everyone is void. There is no point in addressing anyone. Neither can anyone tell where one is from."*

"King Oedipus was accompanied by Theseus when he trudged into the forest. Called by the god, they went to the underworld. But I don't want to go just to watch your death, Father. You should go alone into the forest to look for a ravine, like a sick elephant."

"How has your heart hardened so, while you are still so young?"

"When my body grew this thin, my heart became gaunt and dried out as well. Like mother's." As she said this, Mariko's naked body shone like the blade of a sword.

"She's already a dead tree," Keisaku said, blinded by the gleam. "You're still young, and if you are that thin now, you'll exhaust all your energy and burn away. How did your body get like that?"

---

*A quote from a Noh play *Kagekiyo,* in my translation. An entire translation of this play is included in Arthur Waley, trans. "Kagekiyo," in *The No Plays of Japan* (1921; Tokyo: Tuttle, 1976), 89–99.—trans.

"How? You should know how," Mariko said, wrapping her long hair around Keisaku's neck. Keisaku could scarcely breathe. "What do you want me to do?" he croaked, sounding like a pubescent boy.

"Kill that woman." The thing that said this, pressing its cheek against Keisaku's, was the head of a witch. It had no torso. The crackling voice of a madwoman lingered in Keisaku's ears.

When that voice had died out, there were men's voices at the gate. When he got up and went to look, he found two men standing there. They were samurai, dressed in ancient ceremonial garb. It was clear that they had come to arrest Keisaku and deliver him to the police.

"And you are?" asked Keisaku.

The two men responded in unison, "We are from the travel company. We have come to meet you."

Ridiculous fellows, you don't fool me a bit, thought Keisaku as he donned a priest's hat and robes and stepped outside.

"Will this clothing do?"

"It's fine—though *happi hangiri akujō idetachi* would be better, if it were ever possible."

"How could I dress like the dead?"

As he said this Keisaku followed the two men, who had turned and were heading west, but when they reached the western outskirts of town the road forked, with one branch running to the crematory.

"Enough already. It's time you revealed your true identities," Keisaku said to the men. "You guys are King Emma's messengers, right? The destination has got to be Hell. You'll have me enter Hell from the mouth of the crematorium furnace."

The men exchanged glances, smirking. Suddenly insolent, they replied, "Sir, Hell's not that easy—well, here we are."

Keisaku looked up. Before them was a many-storied building of gold. "What's that," he asked. "Don't you recognize it?" the men sneered. "It's like a school for bodhisattvas." But they seemed to speak uncertainly, and he did not trust them. As they drew closer, what had appeared to be a many-storied building of gold now looked like the crude barracks of the driving school on the outskirts of town. To the left and right of the gate stood two guards, wearing red headbands; their attire seemed to suggest that at present they might be on strike. The guards handed Keisaku a blank form and ordered him to fill in his nationality, address, surname, given name, and date of birth. Then clutching his arms firmly, the two samurai walked Keisaku down the long road. When they had gone a little ways, though there was no fire to be seen, nor was there any sunlight, he felt an intense heat.

"Why's it so hot?" Keisaku asked, and the two men responded, "Yeah, it's pretty hot, isn't it?" as if proud of the fact. "This is hell heat, for roasting you." When they had gone a little farther, suddenly a red-hot iron pillar stood in their path; it looked to Keisaku like a heating device. The men brought Keisaku up to the pillar.

"Okay, hug it." As he did so his flesh instantly burnt and melted away, leaving only his skeleton clinging to the pillar. There was no intense pain, and he remained conscious. That consciousness recognized that what was now happening to him was something he had once read about somewhere, a tale from the second volume of *The Account of Spirits and Miracles in Japan* the "tale of a man of wisdom, who, having envied and spoken ill of a sage, an incarnation of a buddha, was consequently led to King Emma's palace and tormented in Hell while still alive."* The wise man was a man from Kawachi Province, a Buddhist priest from the Sukita temple by the name of Saka Chikō, while the sage was the buddhist novice Gyōgi.

> In his way stood a pillar of extremely hot iron. The messenger ordered, "Embrace it!" Kō accordingly embraced the pillar, and his flesh was all melted and decayed, leaving bones alone. Three days later, the messenger brushed the pillar with a worn broom, saying, "Revive, revive." Then Kō's flesh was restored to him.**

That would be unnecessary, thought Keisaku, he wouldn't need flesh. But his flesh was growing back.

"Enough with the visit to Hell."

"Now, there's an even ghastlier place called Avici."

"Probably more of the same. These places are boring. Isn't there somewhere more interesting?" Keisaku asked.

Fusa handed Mariko the thermometer she had drawn from under the sick man's armpit. Mariko held it up and read it: forty-one degrees. It was as if delusion had raked up all the spiritual material left in this vessel of flesh and set it on fire, burning her father's body.

"Forty-one degrees." As Mariko said this, Keisaku's cousin, the doctor, shook his head slowly. It was as if he had known all along, as if there were no point now in being either cheered or saddened at the temperature.

While the doctor was checking the patient's pulse,

---

*/**Quotes from *Nihon Ryōiki* in my translation. For an entire translation, see Kyoko Motomochi Nakamura, trans. *Miraculous Stories from the Japanese Buddhist Tradition: The Nihon Ryōiki of the Monk Kyōkai.* (Cambridge, MA: Harvard University Press, 1973), 167–71.—trans.

Mariko discreetly inverted her left wrist over and looked at her watch. It was eight fifty.

Thinking the room terribly dark, Mariko looked up, wondering if one of the double-circle fluorescent ceiling lights had gone out, but neither had. She wondered whether more light were not needed when a person died. Given the darkness of the hole he was about to enter, the dying person probably would not even notice a surfeit of light. Far from it—to extinguish the darkness that would seep out of that hole, one might as well tie down a ball of light as big as the sun. But here in this room the power of the darkness was hard to defy—it seemed as if it would gradually suck up all the surrounding light. The room was now gloomy and lonely. The seated figures looked like ghosts. Mariko looked for Takatsu's form among them. She was seeking a youth like Apollo, sole representative of reason, sparkling with an inner light, to send her the message, "Don't lose your sanity!" Takatsu was seated in a corner of the room. He was like one of the narrators on the Noh stage, sitting erect with a fan before his knees and punctuating the conversation between the protagonist and the supporting actor.

As she watched her mother wipe Keisaku's lips with a damp piece of cotton gauze, Mariko supposed that even in her father's final moments, her mother would not cry as she might be expected to. She would certainly never forget herself so far as to throw herself, weeping, onto the dead body. That Mariko was thus convinced meant she could respect her mother. In her early twenties, Mariko had been intoxicated by the notion of love and had used this notion to explain to herself the relationship between her father and her mother. When she had concluded that her mother did not love her father, she had wanted to take her father's side. But the Mariko of today had long since recovered from her infatuation with love, and this father who had once revealed the truth about his relationship with her mother to an intoxicated Mariko now seemed rather odious. Mariko thought her father, including the weak parts he had exposed to her, would probably become dear to her only after he had died and become a departed soul. Her mother, on the other hand, had no such weaknesses. She had become an old witch in the mountains. When Takatsu had written to Mariko after asking her parents for permission to marry her, he had said he would have chosen her mother if she were as young as Mariko. This might be seen as an insult, but Mariko did not get especially upset. Instead, she accepted Takatsu's judgment as only natural. The world of Homer was one in which "it is rare that a son is more excellent than his father, and he is usually worse." Mariko was happy for the same law to apply to mothers and daughters.

As his condition worsened, Keisaku reached a point at which he freely crossed the boundaries between reality and dream. His imaginative powers began to drift without restraint, as his ability to control them deteriorated. His control of his limbs and his mouth deteriorated as well. When Keisaku became conscious of his body's disabilities, he ceased to chant or dance. With his promptbook lying open on his lap, he chewed the muffled words in his mouth like taffies. Liberated—or rather, licentious—he returned to his former self and dared such things as to assume the role of the major character. He would then voice the words of the person whose form he had taken. It was the same as dreaming, but he dreamed in front of others' eyes, whereas one usually dreamt alone, enveloped in a pouch of sleep. The words he blurted out were from dreams. To Fusa's mind, his speech was nonsense. She considered these dreams that leaked out unrestrained by the social conventions of language to be something shameful, like his excreta. Keisaku's status as an invalid dated from the time both his brain and bladder had begun to leak. It was from this time as well that Fusa began addressing Keisaku as "that person" rather than Father in front of the children.

During the rainy season, Keisaku, who had begun to be taken with pneumonia, which gave rise to high fever, escaped the brunt of the disease by means of an antibiotic shot. From this time, however, his condition worsened, and his features turned into those of a person with a fatal illness. He spared few words; the rare ones he emitted were gibberish from dreams. He was no longer able to take up the promptbook as he had often done before the rainy season. He also grew indifferent to the sensory pleasures of television and radio. Keisaku, who slept face up, and displayed an idiotic expression with no link to the outside world even when conscious, was no more than a perpetual dreamer who had somehow survived through the long summer.

The hole he slid into was like an ant lion's trap. The funnel-shaped pit of sand caved in without much resistance, and the sandy bottom collapsed under his feet. Just as he thought his body was floating in mid air, Keisaku passed through the bottom of the hole and came to rest upon new ground. It was like the area of Kumano, and also like Adachigahara, or perhaps the country of Kasuga in Yamato Province. It was a dimly lit world as far as one could see. Keisaku thought the regions where he had tried to travel must be this kind of place. Mariko was not even in his thoughts now. This was a solo trip, and he was a priest glimpsing numerous realms.

Many days passed, and the place he'd now arrived at was an absolutely denuded wasteland, covered with stones.

There was one hovel on the verge of collapse, and a well surrounded by stones beside it. He heard a voice from inside the hovel saying, "Indeed, there is nothing more sad than recluses' lives. Upon the arrival of autumn in such a wretched world, the morning winds do not console my heart, but instead feel intolerable to my body. Another day went by for nothing yesterday, so the midnight when I fall asleep for a while is all that I can hang on to. Alas, what an unstable life."*

On hearing this, Keisaku surmised that the owner of this residence was the witch who dwelt inside the black mound of Adachigahara. Not bothered by this, Keisaku announced his presence. It was an old man who came out, his face the face of the Sankōjō character. That meant his true character was a male demon. Mustn't this be the old field watcher who frequently visited both the mountains and the hamlets of the Plains of Kasuga after he grew old? Keisaku announced his name and formally requested lodging at the inn for one night. Unexpectedly, the old man complied cheerfully with this request and invited Keisaku inside.

"Excuse me, what do you do here? I take you for the field watcher."

"I am the spring watcher," the old man said, staring at Keisaku with pupilless eyes. "Your former self was a dentist, right?" Keisaku was not in the least surprised—a demon should at least be able to perceive that much.

"How many teeth did you pull out?"

"An immense number."

"You should try counting them," the old man said. He stood up and flung open the door to what looked like a

---

*A quote from *Adachigahara,* or *Kurozuka* in another name, a Noh play, in my translation.—trans.

bedchamber. A foul smell immediately filled the air. Keisaku saw a mountain of extracted teeth piled up to the ceiling of the room. Each of the innumerable teeth had a forked root like ginseng, to which clung chunks of gum smirched with blood. Keisaku was utterly at a loss.

"I can't possibly count them," Keisaku said.

"These are the teeth you pulled over a lifetime."

"There are so many even I feel sick. Why would you gather such things?"

"Come with me. I'll show you something really interesting." Saying this, the old man grabbed a handful of teeth from the pile and went out. Keisaku recalled a story Mariko had once told him: if he scattered the teeth on the ground, a troop of armed soldiers would probably spring from the ground and kill each other.

The old man stood by the side of the ruined well.

"Is this a fountain?" Keisaku asked, peering into it. There was no water, but it did not seem to be a dried-up well because it had no bottom. Nor was it dark inside, as one would expect a deep well to be. It was a limitless hole, bounded emptiness.

"This is the well of Prajna Paramita," said the old man. "In other words, the well of perfect knowledge. In this well, once in a few thousand—no, tens of thousands of years, or perhaps an immeasurable span of time, though it could just as well be right now—water will bubble up and serve as a mirror. And then every *rupa,* or *selva dharma* will be perfectly reflected."

"Will it also reflect my image?"

"Your past and future, the past and future of your entire family—and besides that, everyone in this world and their pasts and futures. Everything that existed before this world began and everything that will be after this world has disappeared, will be reflected in this mirror."

"In other words, everything will appear reduced, as if you were looking through the wrong end of a telescope, right?"

"But when you try to look, a hawk wheels down, and breaks the water mirror with its beak," the old man said, and when Keisaku looked at the corner of the sky to which the old man pointed, he made out something like a black speck there. As he watched it drew closer, becoming a huge hawk, which began to circle overhead. The old man scattered the teeth he was holding onto the ground. With a violent rush of its wings, the ominous bird wheeled down and in an instant greedily devoured the teeth.

"Perhaps when the water gushes up in the well, while the hawk is eating teeth like this, you can look at the Prajna Paramita. So, see anything?"

"I can't see a thing."

"You're supposed to see *sunyata*—the void," the old man said, and his face became the *kobeshimi* mask, the face of a demon.

"So you're going to eat me in one gulp?"

"There's no injustice in the way of demons," said the demon.

"I thought that's how it would be."

"I leave you the well. Watch it diligently; it's good to look upon the perfection of wisdom." With this, the demon chanted:

> As he bent down to the earth, Hell became visible first in a crystal mirror eight feet in diameter. The weighing of sins, the torments of sinful beings, beaten by iron rods—all was shown in the mirror. "Indeed, here's a treasure of a clear mirror, which chastises demons for the evils. Now I am

headed back for Hell." Saying this, the demon stamped and stamped, till the earth gaped, and the demon disappeared into the abyss.*

With that the demon vanished. Now Keisaku was the watcher-demon of the spring. What kind of creature was a demon, wondered Keisaku, as he sat down beside the well. A demon, presumably, must be a creature that lives on the boundary between this world and the realm of spirits. It was the nature of the demon, while drawing its transformative powers from the realm of spirits, still to be unable to refrain from eating humans. Such an existence was due to nothing but a flawed peeling-off of flesh from spirit, Keisaku thought. To cast off the attachment to flesh was enough—once that was accomplished, even a deep-rooted delusion that had congealed and taken the form of a demon could escape. The way to the other shore was through this well; only those who had discarded their flesh could hurl themselves into this well and attain Paramita.

The circling hawk's beating wings were as noisy as the pounding of a heart. Throwing a handful of molars as if tossing pebbles, Keisaku tried to distract the hawk and peer into the well's depths. As before, there was no water in the well, nor was a single thing reflected there. This time Keisaku realized that the hope that all things existing in the confinement of time and space might be reflected here in miniature was nothing more than a delusion. What was reflected was the void; in reality, emptiness itself was already reflected there. The moment he thought he saw it, Keisaku

*A quote from *Nomori,* a Noh play attributed to Zeami (1363–1443), in my own translation. An entire translation of the play is included in Royal Tyler, *Pining Wind: A Cycle of No Plays* (Ithaca, NY: Cornell China–Japan Program, 1978), 188–89 as "The Watchman's Mirror."—trans.

felt the hawk's sharp beak in his back. His back split in two, and like a cicada shedding its shell, Keisaku shed his flesh; what remained was the discarded cicada—the husk of a long, deluded dream. From *Tamakazura,* learned when he had first begun to study Noh chanting, the words "Turning away obsession, Tamakazura's soul has attained the jewel of Truth, Tamakazura's soul has attained the jewel of Truth, She has awakened from the long passage of dreams"* sounded in his ears. Keisaku, awakening from his dream, entered the well.

"He is dead," said the doctor. It was a little past nine o'clock.

Takatsu began speaking to Mariko in a low voice in the car on the way back from the crematorium.

"Just now when we were picking up the bones, I remembered the last part of Truffaut's *Jules et Jim.*"

"I remember," Mariko answered in a voice that sounded like it was wrapped in a film. It was a tale about a woman and two men. The woman accompanied one of them in death; the man left behind gathered the bones of the other two after they had been cremated.

On the frame that emerged from the furnace, her father had been reduced to charred and brittle bones. When Mariko saw fragments of spinal column and skull, things with barely a semblance of their original form, remaining in just the same position as when her father lay face up, she

---

*A quote from *Tamakazura,* a Noh play, in my own translation. An entire translation of this play is entitled "The Jewelled Chaplet" and included in Janet Emily Goff, *Noh Drama and* The Tale of Genji: *The Art of Allusion in Fifteen Classical Plays* (Princeton, NJ: Princeton University Press, 1991), 120–24.—trans.

had a feeling that pierced her chest. These were definitely the remains of an animal. They seemed to her like the burnt form of some long reptile rather than the remnants of her father.

Although Mariko was upset with Takatsu for bringing up a movie they had seen together long ago at a time like this, she also understood his motive. She knew he meant merely to break the silence with his story and unlock her hardened heart. In this understanding was also included thanks. If this was the kind of person Takatsu was, she supposed she would not hate him, though she would not love him either. Takatsu had wanted to marry Mariko and as a result had become involved in her father's death. After this, his will to marry her would surely also wither; more than for any other reason, Mariko had decided this because she herself had become like a broken doll. But she had never thought of relying on Takatsu to help gather her scattered limbs and head and put them back together. With regard to Takatsu's sense of responsibility for bringing on the first symptoms of her father's illness, to say: "You weren't responsible," or "I forgive you," or even "I can't forgive you" would be to use him to rebuild her shattered self. But that was something Mariko could not do.

Before she was aware of it, her hands were seized by Takatsu's. She surrendered her hands—which seemed almost to belong to the dead person—to Takatsu, as they grew moist with perspiration.

The car ascended the slope before the bridge, carrying her head into the depths of the blue sky.

She said, "This weather is more than the funeral deserves." At that moment the land, the mountains, and the rows of houses and stores disappeared from her vision and she could see only sky before her. A feeling that her broken self had become whole again came back to Mariko. From the joints where she had been put back together into her former self, she sensed a sweet sorrow seeping for the first time. She knew Takatsu saw the tears under her closed eyelids. Blood began to circulate through the hands that had died. Blood seemed to rise from her neck, and her face, which had been paralyzed, came drowsily back to life. She felt as if the life she lived with all her might up to now had been like one long dream.

Mariko thought that in time she would be able to talk about marriage with Takatsu—and what kind of reply would she give then? As she thought, I'm still not sure, Mariko listened for her father's voice. By grasping Takatsu's hand with all her strength at the moment the car approached the bridge, she intended to indicate that she had heard it.

List of Japanese Sources of the Translated Works

---

1. "Uchūjin." 1964. *Kurahashi Yumiko zensakuhin* [*Complete Works of Kurahashi Yumiko*]. Vol. 4. Shinchōsha, 1976. 185–207.
2. "Koibito dōshi." 1963. *Kurahashi Yumiko zensakuhin*. Vol. 4. 95–104.
3. "Kuroneko no ie." 1989. *Yume no kayoiji*. Kōdansha, 1989. 103–10.
4. "Kubi no tobu onna." 1985. *Kurahashi Yumiko no kaiki shōhen*. Shinchō bunko, 1988. 29–38.
5. "Kōkan." 1985. *Kurahashi Yumiko no kaiki shōhen*. 128–38.
6. "Kijo no men." 1985. *Kurahashi Yumiko no kaiki shōhen*. 99–108.
7. "Haru no yo no yume." 1989. *Yume no kayoiji*. 183–95.
8. "Yume no kayoiji." 1988. *Yume no kayoiji*. 213–29.
9. "Erabareta basho." 1988. *Gensō kaigakan*. Bungei shunjū, 1991. 53–60.
10. "Furawā abusutorakushon." 1991. *Gensō kaigakan*. 149–56.
11. "Nagai yumeji." 1968. *Kurahashi Yumiko zensakuhin*. Vol. 6. 1976. 235–70.

About the Author

Kurahashi Yumiko, the original author of *The Adventures of Sumiyakist Q* (translated by Dennis Keene), is renowned for intellectual qualities comparable to those of Franz Kafka and Abe Kōbō demonstrated in her short stories, essays, and novels. She has been awarded several literary prizes, including Joryū bungaku shō (Women's Literary Prize), Tamura Toshiko shō (Tamura Toshiko Prize), and Izumi Kyōka shō (Izumi Kyōka Prize).

About the Translator

Atsuko Sakaki is Associate Professor of Japanese Literature in the Department of East Asian Languages and Civilizations at Harvard University. Her publications include *Kōi to shite no shōsetsu* (Shin'yōsha, 1996), *Ibuse bungaku no honshitsu* (Translation of Anthony Liman's book on Ibuse Masuji; Meiji shoin, 1994), and a number of English and Japanese articles on Kurahashi Yumiko and others. She is finishing a book manuscript in English on the contextuality of narration in prose fiction by Sōseki, Ōgai, Tanizaki, and Ibuse.

About the Author

About the Translator